Make Sh** Happen

How to Release REAL Power into Your Life

Deborah LeBlanc, CCHt, CAHA

Copyright © 2023 Deborah LeBlanc, CCHt, CAHA

All rights reserved.

The contents of this book may not be reproduced, duplicated, or transmitted without direct written permission from the author.

Under no circumstances will any legal responsibility or blame be held against the publisher for any reparation, damages, or monetary loss due to the information herein, either directly or indirectly.

Legal Notice:

This book is copyright-protected. This is only for personal use. You cannot amend, distribute, sell, use, quote, or paraphrase any part of the content within this book without the consent of the author.

Disclaimer Notice:

Please note the information contained within this document is for educational and entertainment purposes only. Every attempt has been made to provide accurate, up-to-date, reliable, and complete information. No warranties of any kind are expressed or implied. Readers acknowledge that the author is not engaging in the rendering of legal, financial, medical, or professional advice. The content of this book has been derived from various sources. Please consult a licensed professional before attempting any techniques outlined in this book.

By reading this document, the reader agrees that under no circumstances is the author responsible for any losses, direct or indirect, which are incurred as a result of the use of the information contained within this document, including, but not limited to, errors, omissions, or inaccuracies.

ISBN: 978-1-937209-17-9

Contents

Introduction 1
1. The Power of Mindset 5
   The Enigmatic Influence of Mindset
   Mindset: A Scientific Discourse
   Mindset in Practice
2. The Science of Motivation—Unveiling the Why behind 11
   Your Actions
   Extrinsic Motivation
   Intrinsic Motivation
   Importance of Motivation
   The Three Components of Motivation—Activation, Persistence, and Intensity
   Science-Backed Strategies to Improve Motivation
   Conclusion
3. Setting Epic Goals 25
   Strategies for Effective Goal Setting
   The Significance of Goal Setting in Your Life
   Common Goal-Setting Pitfalls
   Setting Achievable Goals for Sustained Success
   Conclusion

4. Overcoming Procrastination with Laughs 39
   Psychologists' View of Procrastination
   The Negative Impact of Procrastination
   Strategies for Overcoming Procrastination
   Conclusion

5. Hacking Productivity with a Sense of Humor 51
   The Essence of Time Management
   Strategies for Enhancing Productivity
   Conclusion

6. Navigating Obstacles with a Grin 65
   The Many Faces of Challenges
   Financial Hurdles and Relationship Mazes
   Academic and Professional Obstacles
   Confronting the Dragon of Fear
   You Are Not Alone
   The Healing Power of Laughter
   Laughter: A Universal Currency
   Scientific Insights into Laughter
   Laughter as a Social Glue
   Laughter is the Best Medicine
   Incorporating Laughter into Your Life
   Tackling Challenges with Grace
   Managing Stress and Anxiety
   Celebrating Accomplishments
   Understanding Perseverance
   The Role of Perseverance in Learning and Mastery
   Personality Traits and Perseverance
   Perseverance as a Character Strength: Grit
   Grit in Academic and Professional Contexts

Developing Grit and Perseverance
The Psychology of Resilience
Characteristics of Resilient Individuals
Building a Resilient Mindset
Conclusion

7. The Art of Networking and Building Relationships — 82
Understanding Networking
The Purpose of Networking
Keys to Effective Networking
Importance of Healthy Social Relationships in Achieving Goals
The Underestimated Power of Support Systems
Engaging Others in Your Goal Journey
The Role of Specificity in Accountability
Building a Network for Success
Tips for Building Lasting Connections
The Benefits of Networking
The Networking Ecosystem
Conclusion

8. Cultivating Grit and Determination — 97
The Power of Grit and Determination
Understanding Grit and Determination
The Relationship between Grit and Determination
The Crucial Role of Grit and Determination in Achieving Success
Real-Life Examples of Grit and Determination
Developing Grit and Determination: Your Path to Success
Conclusion

9. Celebrating Success with a Chuckle — 112
Why Celebrate Success?

Physiological Benefits of Celebrating Success
Setting Goals and Defining Success
Celebrating vs. Rewarding
Celebrating Success in a Healthy Way
Enjoy the Journey
You Have Permission to Have Fun
Focus on Progress and Celebrate Small Victories
Embracing Challenges, Risks, and Mistakes: Finding Joy in the Journey
Slow and Steady Wins the Race
The Journey Teaches You to Be Adaptable
Conclusion

10. Take Risks and Make Sh** Happen   127

Introduction

Buckle up, dreamers hoping to be doers. This book is a no-nonsense guide for those who've planned it all but done little. Here, we strip away the surface and expose the core of what drives change—your mindset. This book is for anyone who's ever felt like they're on the cusp of something great but can't seem to take that pivotal step. It's for the serial planners, the perpetual "getting ready to get ready" crowd, and the folks poised to make sh** happen... who need that final (gentle) shove into taking action.

You're about to embark on a journey that's about lighting a fire in you. You'll navigate the mental and psychological puzzles that keep you from tapping into your full potential. This book is the sage old mechanic to the race car driver that is your will—you've got the drive, but perhaps the engine hasn't been firing on all cylinders. That's your mindset, and you're about to tune it up to win races, not just to compete.

Why does this book matter, especially to you? Picture your personal development journey as a road trip. You've plotted the course, packed the essentials, and revved the engine, but there's a catch—your handbrake is still engaged. This book is about releasing that brake and rolling forward.

In this book, you won't find recycled platitudes or motivational clichés. Instead, you'll find a series of candid conversations, frank advice, and tough love, all grounded in psychological research and real-world results. This is a boot camp for your brain, designed to help you break out of your way and start making strides.

Chapter by chapter, you will cut through the illusion and put you on a path to start making positive progress in your life. You'll begin by exploring the power of your mindset and how you can develop a doer's mentality. In the second chapter, you'll deconstruct the myths that have held you back. Also, you'll learn how to navigate around the distractions that have previously limited you from reaching your potential. And by the time you get to the last chapter, you'll not only have the map but also the determination to reach your destination.

But what's knowledge without application? Fear not. This book contains exercises, anecdotes, and insights that won't just tickle your fancy but will also challenge you to plan and act. You will be equipped with not just the "why" but also the "how" to set the wheels in motion with a strategic plan tailored to your life.

And when the going gets tough—as it inevitably does on the path to greatness—you'll find your reserve of resilience, grit, and tenacity multiplying. You'll not only expect setbacks but welcome them as the fuel for your fire, transforming each challenge into a stepping-stone toward your ultimate goal.

In this book, you'll learn how to harness the formidable power of mindset to move from inertia to action, crafting a life of purposeful achievement with less strain and more satisfaction. Using enlightening anecdotes and a dash of humor, you'll explore how to effectively set goals that resonate with your deepest aspirations and devise a foolproof plan to attain them.

Moreover, you'll learn the art of managing procrastination, transforming it from a hindrance into a tool for strategic pacing. You will also discover the importance of motivation, as it enables you to fuel your drive with precision and persistence.

Next, you'll demystify the principles of productivity, equipping you with time-management hacks that are as enjoyable as they are effective, ensuring that you can do more with less while enjoying every step of the journey. You'll learn to navigate life's unpredictable challenges with resilience, finding humor in adversity, which not only makes obstacles more manageable but also less daunting.

The book will show you how to expand your network and enrich your relationships, which can be the most fulfilling part of your adventure toward success. Additionally, you'll learn to cultivate a spirit of grit and determination. Life's challenges are inevitable, but it is your ability to persevere, to face adversity head-on, and to transform setbacks into stepping-stones that will truly set you apart. Through the wisdom contained in these pages, you will gain the strength to endure where others might falter, allowing you to navigate the complexities of life with grace and resilience.

And finally, you'll discover the importance of celebrating your successes—no matter how small—with a heart full of joy and a mind keen on the next adventure. Each step on this path is designed with one goal in mind—and you already know what that is! So, whether you're the CEO of a startup, a stay-at-home parent with a vision, or a writer with a half-written novel, this book is your manifesto. It's your permission slip to cut through the noise, do things your way, and succeed with a spring in your step and a chuckle in your throat.

You won't finish this book as a different person, but you will have evolved. You'll have gained a personalized toolkit for change, built not on the sands of wishful thinking but on the solid ground of action-oriented psychology. It's about honing a mindset that doesn't just acknowledge your potential but actively chases it down, tackles it, and puts it to work.

As you turn the final page, you won't just close a book—you'll open a door to a new way of living. You'll have evolved from a dreamer to a doer, planner to a conqueror. Armed with a newfound understanding and many tools that render the difficult simple, you'll be ready to make sh** happen, transforming minimal effort into maximum satisfaction.

So, fluff up your reading pillow, grab your highlighter or your beverage of choice, and prepare for a journey that promises not only to guide you to your goals but to redefine the very way you approach them. This is your time, your turn, and your book. Let's tune up that engine and drive your aspirations from imagination to the solid, sweet ground of reality.

Chapter One
The Power of Mindset

Welcome to a journey that's all about helping you go from dreaming and waiting to actually take action and, well, making sh** happen! Whether you've been putting things off or just hoping for a change, this book will guide you in becoming more proactive and successful. Your mindset, as we'll explore in greater depth, is like the captain of your mental ship. It can steer you toward the treacherous waters of self-doubt, procrastination, and missed opportunities, or it can chart a course toward the calm seas of confidence, determination, and achievement. You'll unravel the science behind this mindset phenomenon, revealing that it's not just a matter of positive thinking—it's a cognitive shift that can mold your reality.

The Enigmatic Influence of Mindset

Let's consider the human mind as a unique kind of microwave—a "mindset microwave," if you will. It's a microwave with a twist—it doesn't just heat up food, but it can also heat up or cool down your life based on what you put into it. When you load it up with negativity, doubt, and self-pity, it's like preparing a meal that's been left in the microwave for too long—it turns into a sorry, unappetizing mess. Your life can end up feeling repetitive and stagnant, much like that overcooked dish.

On the flip side, when you feed your "mindset microwave" with positivity, self-assurance, and unwavering determination, it's as if you're concocting a culinary masterpiece that's synonymous with achievement. Likewise, tour life becomes a delicious dish worth savoring.

The mindset isn't just a passive observer—it's the master chef behind the scenes, orchestrating your cognitive landscape. As you delve deeper into this concept, you'll discover that it's not a mere metaphor—it's a potent instrument that can drive profound transformation. This perspective isn't founded on whims but solid empirical research from the field of psychology.

Mindset: A Scientific Discourse

In the realm of personal development and achievement, the concept of mindset stands as a beacon of profound significance. Not just a buzzword or a fleeting self-help fad—it's a dynamic force that can shape the course of our lives. Dr. Carol Dweck, a renowned psychologist and professor at Stanford University, has made significant contributions to our understanding of mindset. Her pioneering work has placed her at the forefront of research in this field. She introduced the groundbreaking concepts of the "fixed mindset" and the "growth mindset," which have become central to the discourse on human potential and achievement. Dweck's insights have provided you with invaluable tools to navigate the complex terrain of the human psyche and have far-reaching implications for personal and professional development. As you journey through the scientific discourse of mindset, her work will serve as a guiding light, illuminating the path toward a deeper comprehension of our cognitive landscapes and their role in your pursuit of success.

Individuals with a *fixed mindset* tend to view their abilities and intelligence as unchangeable and rigid, akin to immovable blocks. In contrast, proponents of the *growth mindset* enthusiastically embrace challenges, viewing failures not as dead ends but as stepping-stones toward progress. They also recognize the critical role of persistent effort in pursuing their goals. From their perspective, competence and intelligence are qualities that can be cultivated and enhanced through unrelenting dedication.

This divergence between fixed and growth mindsets can be humorously characterized by comparing those with a fixed mindset to stubborn toddlers repeatedly exclaiming, "I cannot." This repetitive declaration, unfortunately, sets the stage for a self-fulfilling prophecy of inadequacy. Alternatively, enthusiasts of the growth mindset resemble exuberant children in a candy store, eager to embark on the delightful adventures life has to offer. Here are three more examples to understand the difference between the two types of mindsets:

"I'm Just Not Good at This" vs. "I Can Develop My Skills"—Someone with a fixed mindset believes that their abilities and intelligence are unchangeable, leading them to avoid taking on new challenges or responsibilities. In contrast, individuals with a growth mindset see challenges as opportunities for personal growth and believe that, with effort and the right strategies, they can improve their abilities over time.

"I Don't Take Feedback Well" vs. "Feedback Helps Me Improve"—In a fixed mindset, feedback can be viewed as a threat to self-esteem, causing defensiveness and reluctance to accept constructive criticism. Conversely, those with a growth mindset value feedback as a means to enhance their skills and are open to constructive criticism, understanding that it can lead to personal and professional development.

"I Give Up Easily" vs. "I Persevere through Challenges"—A fixed mindset can lead to frustration and giving up when faced with challenges, whether they are personal projects or career aspirations. Individuals with a growth mindset are more likely to persevere through difficulties, whether it's completing a challenging project at work, pursuing further education, or overcoming personal setbacks.

The crucial lesson here is that mindset is *not* a fixed attribute. It is, in fact, malleable, capable of being reshaped and restructured. Transitioning from a "can't-do" perspective to a "can-do" mindset is a viable transformation.

Mindset in Practice

In the realm of personal and professional growth, the power of mindset often lies in its practical application. It's the bridge between theory and action, where the rubber meets the road on your journey to success. Let's check out some real-life examples and strategies that showcase the incredible impact of mindset in the pursuit of one's goals.

Meet Colonel Sanders, the visionary who gave us Kentucky Fried Chicken (KFC). At the age of sixty-five, he set out on a journey to pitch his secret chicken recipe to over a thousand doors. What fueled his success? *A growth mindset*. His unwavering determination and resilience served as the recipe not only for finger-licking chicken but for a fulfilling life.

But before Colonel Sanders became the iconic face of KFC, he had a colorful array of experiences in his early life. In a way, his journey to success was paved with diverse roles and challenges that ultimately led him to create the globally renowned fried chicken franchise.

Sanders was not born into a life of privilege or culinary expertise. In fact, he started his working life as a steam engine stoker, shoveling coal into the fiery heart of those massive locomotives. His journey took him through various occupations, including stints as an insurance salesman and a filling station operator. It wasn't until the midst of the Great Depression that Sanders began to cook up the recipe for his legendary fried chicken. In North Corbin, Kentucky, he opened a humble roadside restaurant where he started serving his unique and delectable fried chicken to passing travelers. It was a modest beginning, but the taste was extraordinary.

The secret to his success lay in his approach to food. He believed in simple, honest ingredients and a deep commitment to quality. Sanders' fried chicken quickly gained a reputation for its finger-licking goodness. It wasn't long before word-of-mouth and his dedication to perfection turned this small enterprise into a local treasure.

But what set Sanders apart was not just his culinary skills—it was his relentless pursuit of improvement. He was always tinkering with his recipe, trying to make it better. He'd listen to his customers' feedback and make adjustments accordingly. This innovative spirit, coupled with an unyielding determination, eventually led him to perfect the "Original Recipe" of KFC that you know today.

Colonel Sanders' journey is a testament to the power of resilience, adaptability, and an unwavering commitment to quality. It's a reminder that success can come from unexpected places and that even in the toughest times, there's room for a great idea to flourish. It's also a reminder that no matter where you start in life, with the right mindset, the pursuit of excellence can lead to extraordinary achievements.

Now, let's consider Thomas Edison, the inventor who famously said, "I have not failed. I've just found 10,000 ways that won't work." This embodies the essence of a growth mindset. Edison's relentless pursuit of the perfect light bulb wasn't just about brightening rooms—it was about the brilliance of a mindset that refuses to surrender to defeat. But this achievement didn't come easy. In fact, it was marked by countless setbacks and failures.

Edison's mindset, however, was not one that allowed these failures to define him. Instead, he viewed each setback as a valuable lesson. He saw every attempt that didn't result in a working light bulb as a step closer to his ultimate goal. This perspective was at the core of his success.

His relentless work ethic and commitment to innovation were truly astounding. Edison spent years experimenting with various materials and designs for the light bulb, often toiling late into the night in his laboratory. He didn't view any of these efforts as failures but as essential parts of the learning process.

In a sense, he believed that every "failed" attempt brought him one step closer to the solution. His growth mindset allowed him to remain undeterred by the enormity of the task and the seemingly endless challenges. He was not willing to surrender to the countless setbacks, and this determination made all the difference.

These stories serve as beacons of hope and inspiration for anyone seeking to make a meaningful stride toward success. It's not just about seeing the glass as half full—it's about being willing to refill it, over and over again, no matter how many times it appears to be empty. As you embark on your journey, remember that every door you knock on brings you one step closer to the success you desire. So, prepare to harness your inner brilliance, and let the stories of these remarkable individuals be a source of motivation on your way to success.

Chapter Two

The Science of Motivation—Unveiling the Why behind Your Actions

Motivation is the invisible yet powerful force that propels you forward in your quest for achievement and fulfillment. Motivation is much more than a simple term—it's the force that drives your actions, fueling your journey from merely having dreams to manifesting them.

Motivation is the wind in the sails of a mighty ship, steering you toward your desired destination. It's not just a temporary gust—it's a consistent, guiding breeze that helps you navigate through the treacherous seas of life's challenges. This force is what initiates your actions, steers your course toward goals, and keeps you steadfast on this path, regardless of the challenges you encounter.

You can also see motivation as a personal compass, pointing you in the direction of your goals. It's what gets you out of bed in the morning with a heart full of purpose. It's the spark that lights the fire of your aspirations, transforming the mundane into the extraordinary.

In other words, motivation is an intricate dance of internal desires and external stimuli. It's a complex symphony where your deepest passions, fears, and aspirations play in harmony with the opportunities and challenges that the world presents to you.

But what really fuels this powerful force? At its core, motivation is about understanding your "why." It's the underlying reason that gives meaning to your actions. Whether it's the aspiration to excel in your career, the desire to build meaningful relationships, or the pursuit of personal growth, your "why" is the cornerstone of your motivation.

Moreover, motivation is not a static entity—it's a dynamic and evolving process. It adapts and morphs in response to your changing needs, aspirations, and circumstances. It's the guiding light that helps you find your direction when you're lost and the gentle nudge that encourages you to take that leap of faith when opportunities knock on your doors.

In this chapter, you will explore the complex nature of motivation. You'll uncover how it shapes your perceptions, influences your decisions, and, ultimately, dictates the course of your life. From the smallest daily tasks to the grandest of life's goals, motivation is the key that unlocks the door to potential and possibility.

So, buckle up and prepare for an enlightening journey to have a full understanding of motivation. It's time to discover the true essence of this force and learn how to harness its power to transform your life. This exploration will not only provide insights into how motivation works but also offer practical strategies to amplify it, ensuring that you are always moving forward, making sh** happen, fueled by a purpose that resonates with your deepest aspirations.

Extrinsic Motivation

Extrinsic motivation is the bright spotlight, illuminating the rewards and recognitions that await you from the external world. This type of motivation is like a cheering crowd, pushing you toward achievements that are visible and tangible. It's the applause you receive after a stunning performance, the trophy you lift high after a hard-fought victory, and the bonus you earn for surpassing your targets at work. These rewards—trophies, money, social recognition, praise—are the glittering jewels that the world bestows upon you for your efforts and accomplishments.

But extrinsic motivation is more than just a chase for material rewards. It's a combination of societal expectations and norms. It's about earning the respect of your peers, pleasing your loved ones, and carving a niche for yourself in society. This type of motivation is often the fuel behind your quest for excellence in your professional life, your drive to achieve societal status, and your endeavors to fulfill the roles that society has set for you.

Intrinsic Motivation

Now, turn inward and discover intrinsic motivation—the silent, powerful current that flows from the depths of your own psyche. This is the motivation that arises not from external rewards but from the sheer joy and satisfaction of the activity itself. It's the quiet pleasure of engaging in a hobby, the thrill of solving a complex problem, or the serene contentment of peaceful gratification.

Intrinsic motivation is like a personal song, where your deepest passions and interests create a melody that resonates with your core. It's the internal drive that compels an artist to paint not for fame or fortune but for the love of painting itself. It's the force that drives a scientist to spend hours in a lab not for accolades but for the sheer thrill of discovery. This type of motivation comes from doing things that align with your personal values, interests, and passions, providing a sense of fulfillment and contentment that external rewards cannot match.

In life, extrinsic and intrinsic motivations are not isolated—instead, they are interwoven threads that together fuel your actions and experiences. Sometimes, you find yourself driven by external rewards and recognitions, propelled by the desire to meet societal expectations or to attain material success. Other times, you are moved by the inner joy and satisfaction derived from an activity, independent of any external praise or reward.

As you journey through this chapter, you will explore how these two types of motivation interact and influence each other. Through this exploration, you will learn to recognize the forces that motivate you and how to harness them to live a life that is not only successful but also rich in personal fulfillment and joy.

Importance of Motivation

Why is motivation such a critical element in your life? Let's explore the different ways in which it serves as a force, getting you through each day and guiding you toward a life of efficiency, action, health, and well-being.

Elevating Efficiency in Pursuit of Goals

Think of motivation as the fuel in your car on the journey toward your goals. When you understand what drives you, you can tap into this energy source more effectively, propelling you forward with greater efficiency and purpose. This understanding transforms your efforts from wandering explorations into targeted, strategic actions, significantly enhancing your ability to reach your desired destinations with precision and speed.

Igniting the Spark of Action

Motivation is the spark that ignites action. It's the force that nudges you from contemplation to making sh** happen. When you grasp the essence of what motivates you, you're more likely to leap into action, turning your visions and dreams into tangible realities.

Promoting Health-Oriented Behaviors

Consider motivation as your personal health coach, encouraging you to engage in behaviors that nurture your physical, mental, and emotional well-being. Understanding your motivational drivers can lead you to adopt healthier lifestyles, make wiser health choices, and pursue activities that enhance your overall well-being. It's the inner voice that encourages you to choose a salad over fast food, to take that morning jog, or to meditate for mental clarity.

Help You Avoid Unhealthy Behaviors

Just as a lighthouse warns ships of dangerous shores, motivation helps steer clear of unhealthy or maladaptive behaviors. By understanding what motivates these behaviors—whether it's risk-taking, addiction, or other harmful practices—you gain the power to redirect your energies toward more constructive and positive endeavors. This insight is crucial in navigating away from harmful habits and toward a safer, healthier lifestyle.

Cultivating a Sense of Control over Life

Imagine holding the reins of a magnificent horse, guiding it wherever you wish to go. Similarly, understanding your motivations gives you a sense of control over the direction of your life. It empowers you to make decisions that align with your values and goals, giving you a feeling of autonomy and mastery over your destiny.

Enhancing Overall Well-Being and Happiness

Motivation is the sunlight that nurtures the garden of your life, allowing joy, satisfaction, and well-being to bloom. By understanding and harnessing your motivational forces, you create an environment conducive to personal growth and happiness. This understanding not only elevates your sense of fulfillment but also radiates outward, positively impacting those around you.

The Three Components of Motivation—Activation, Persistence, and Intensity

In your journey to understand motivation, it's essential to recognize that it's not a singular entity. Instead, motivation comprises three vital components that work in harmony to propel you toward your goals. These three components—activation, persistence, and intensity—are the gears that power the engine of motivation, driving you forward in your quest for success and fulfillment.

Activation: The Spark of Beginning

Activation is the initial spark that ignites the flame of action. It's the moment you decide to take the first step toward your goal. Imagine standing at the foot of a mountain, gazing up at its peak. Activation is that deep breath you take before you start your ascent. It's the decision to enroll in a course, sign up for a marathon, or begin a weight loss program. This initial commitment is the foundation upon which the journey toward any goal is built.

Persistence: The Strength to Continue

If activation is the spark, persistence is the fuel that keeps the fire burning. It's the sustained effort and determination to keep moving forward, despite the obstacles and challenges that inevitably arise. Persistence is what keeps you attending those psychology classes even when you're exhausted, what drives you to keep running even when your legs feel like they're made of lead. It's the unwavering commitment to your goal, the refusal to give up even when the path becomes steep and treacherous.

Intensity: The Power Behind the Pursuit

Finally, intensity is the vigor and concentration you pour into your pursuit. It's not just about staying the course; it's about how you navigate it. Intensity is the difference between going through the motions and striving with purpose and passion. It's what separates the student who barely skims through their course material from the one who dives deep into their studies, engages in class discussions, and seeks out additional learning opportunities. Intensity is about the quality of effort, not just the quantity.

Each of these components plays a critical role in getting you motivated. Activation gets you started on your journey, persistence helps you overcome the hurdles along the way, and intensity determines the quality and effectiveness of your efforts.

Science-Backed Strategies to Improve Motivation

Embarking on a journey to achieve your goals, be it earning a degree, landing a dream job, or reaching a new level of fitness, is a commendable endeavor that can profoundly enhance your life. However, the path to achieving these aspirations is often strewn with challenges, and maintaining a steady stream of motivation can sometimes feel like navigating through a dense fog. How do you keep the fire of commitment burning during those inevitable moments when your motivation seems to dim?

When you find yourself in a motivational slump, there are scientifically proven strategies to reignite your drive and get back on track toward your goal.

Calendarize Your Goals

Transform your internal drive into external momentum by marking your target date on a calendar. Whether it's a fixed deadline like a test date or a self-imposed milestone, having a concrete date creates a sense of urgency and commitment. This strategy is more than just a mental trick; it's a way to visually track your progress, giving you a clear view of how far you've come and how much further you need to go. Research shows that having a definitive timeline can significantly boost your performance.

Setting a Target Date: Be pragmatic yet ambitious when setting your target date. Interestingly, studies indicate that longer timelines can sometimes be perceived as more daunting, potentially leading to procrastination or even abandonment of the goal. So, aim for a balance—realistic yet challenging enough to keep you engaged and motivated.

Make Working toward Your Goal a Habit

Transforming your goal-oriented actions into habits can reduce the reliance on fluctuating motivation levels. How do you turn a behavior into a habit? Start by identifying a daily routine as a trigger and create an "if-then" plan. This could be as simple as, "If I pour my morning coffee, then I'll spend five minutes on my math homework." The key is to link a new, goal-directed action to an established habit.

Start Small: The initial step doesn't have to be monumental. It's about overcoming the fear of starting. A small action, like studying for five minutes or donning workout clothes, can be enough to set the stage for more substantial efforts. These initial steps help prime your mind, making the transition to more extensive tasks feel more natural and less daunting.

Anticipate and Plan for Challenges

The art of maintaining motivation lies not only in striving for perfection but also in planning for imperfection. Consider the potential roadblocks you might encounter. For instance, if you're taking an online course, challenges could include losing internet access, unexpected interruptions, or grappling with tough concepts. If your goal is daily running, obstacles might range from bad weather to work demands. While you can't foresee every hurdle, understanding and preparing for common challenges can keep you from being derailed.

Creating a Contingency Plan: Once you've identified potential obstacles, devise a plan to navigate them. If internet issues could disrupt your studies, have offline resources ready. If your running schedule could be upset by weather or work, plan alternative workout times or indoor exercises. By preparing for these challenges, you transform them from motivation busters into manageable bumps in the road.

The WOOP Method: A powerful tool in goal setting is the WOOP method, developed by Dr. Gabriele Oettingen. This technique involves four steps: Wish, Outcome, Obstacle, and Plan. First, identify your wish (the goal). Then, envision the outcome (the benefits of achieving this goal). Next, recognize the main obstacles that might stand in your way. Finally, create a plan to overcome these obstacles. This method not only helps in visualizing success but also prepares you for the challenges along the way.

Set Smaller, Achievable Goals

Author and U.S. four-star Admiral William H. McRaven says that beginning each morning by making your bed is a testament to the power of small victories. These minor successes create a sense of momentum, propelling you toward larger achievements. Break down your overarching goal into smaller, manageable tasks. For instance, if your goal is to get a new job, start with updating your resumé, creating a portfolio, earning a certification, or attending a networking event. Research suggests that these small wins, especially early on, can build a foundation for long-term success.

Leverage Temporal Landmarks for Motivation: Interestingly, the start of a new week, month, or year can boost motivation. You tend to view these moments as fresh starts, a chance to leave past shortcomings behind and embark on new endeavors. Embrace these temporal landmarks as opportunities for renewed energy and focus. Utilize them to set new goals or recommit to ongoing ones, capitalizing on this natural surge in motivation.

Utilize Goal-Tracking Tools

The act of tracking progress is not just a ritual; it's a catalyst for motivation. For some, a traditional to-do list or calendar suffices, offering the satisfaction of crossing off completed tasks. Others might prefer digital solutions like Trello, which allow for a more dynamic and interactive way of organizing and visualizing progress. These tools can be customized to break down a larger goal into smaller, more manageable segments—daily, weekly, monthly, or yearly tasks—making the journey toward your goal seem less daunting and more structured.

Create a Visual Progress Indicator: Another effective strategy is to create a visual representation of your progress. Drawing a progress bar on a poster board and placing it in a prominent location can serve as a constant, tangible reminder of how far you've come and how close you are to achieving your goal. Each time you fill in a section of the bar, it's a visual celebration of your persistence and dedication.

Celebrate Both Small and Large Victories

The journey toward a goal is made up of countless steps, and each step, no matter how small, deserves recognition. Rewarding yourself for both minor milestones and major achievements can significantly enhance your motivation and enjoyment of the task at hand. Remember, rewards need not be extravagant, but they should simply be things that bring you joy and rejuvenation.

Here are some ideas for self-rewards:

- Take a brief, relaxing break to clear your mind.
- Immerse yourself in the tranquility of nature with a walk outside.
- Indulge in your favorite snack as a treat for your efforts.
- Dive into the world of your favorite book for a chapter or two.
- Engage in a few minutes of meditation to center your thoughts.
- Listen to an episode of a podcast you love.
- Plan an enjoyable night out with friends to celebrate your hard work.

- Enjoy a session of an online game to unwind.

- Visit a free museum or attraction to stimulate your mind in new ways.

- Indulge in the luxury of a long bath or an invigorating shower.

- Connect with a loved one through a phone call.

Personalize your reward list, ensuring that you have a repertoire of celebrations ready for every achievement, big or small.

The Power of Gratitude

Gratitude extends beyond a simple "thank you." It's a profound appreciation that can significantly impact our motivation and overall well-being. Studies have shown that gratitude can fuel self-improvement, foster a sense of community and teamwork, sustain motivation over time, inspire a desire to give back, and improve both physical and mental health, including better sleep quality.

Implementing Gratitude Practices: There are various ways to cultivate gratitude. One effective method is to spend the first few minutes after waking up reflecting on what you're grateful for. Writing these thoughts in a gratitude journal can further reinforce this positive mindset. Additionally, expressing gratitude to others, such as writing a thank-you letter to someone who has made a difference in your life, can deepen your sense of appreciation and connection.

Boosting Mood for Productivity and Motivation

A positive mood is linked to increased productivity and enhanced quality and quantity of work. Think about the last time you went to work feeling excited to be there. Did you get a lot of work done? Were you able to work efficiently with your coworkers? Now, picture the last time you went to work with a thundercloud over your head. Did the day feel like it was dragging on? Did you make a lot of mistakes that you had to re-do the next day? While it's unrealistic to expect to be in high spirits all the time, lifting your mood when feeling sluggish can be just the push needed to get started on your goals.

There are several ways to elevate your mood. Spending time in nature or soaking up some sunlight can have a rejuvenating effect. Viewing cute animal pictures on platforms like Reddit's r/aww or watching humorous videos on YouTube can offer a quick mood lift. Engaging in physical exercise is also a proven mood enhancer.

Additionally, the concept of adopting an alter ego—the "Batman effect"—can empower you to tackle tasks with renewed vigor and perspective. Don't worry; the Batman effect doesn't require you to don a cap and spend your nights fighting supervillains. Instead, it allows you to create an alternate persona or a mask that you can wear in challenging situations. In fact, many famous musicians use this technique when performing: Beyonce with Sasha Fierce and Adele with Sasha Carter. This alter ego allows you to distance yourself from hard-to-handle emotions and gives you the ability to move through your day with the confidence of DC's greatest detective or a world-renowned pop star. Imagine walking into work with that energy. Wow.

Conclusion

As you reach the conclusion of your exploration of motivation, it's important to pause and reflect on the journey you've undertaken. From understanding the essence of motivation to employing practical strategies for sustaining it, this exploration has been a deep dive into the heart of what drives you forward in pursuit of your goals and aspirations.

Throughout this chapter, you've uncovered the complex nature of motivation—its components, the significance of planning for imperfections, the art of tracking progress, and the profound impact of gratitude and mood elevation. This chapter has offered insights and tools designed to enhance your motivation, equipping you with the knowledge and strategies to navigate the ups and downs of your personal and professional endeavors.

As you conclude, remember that the journey of motivation is ongoing. It's a continuous process of learning, adapting, and growing. The strategies and insights provided in these chapters are not just tools for achieving specific goals—they are guides for a lifetime of motivation and personal growth.

The path to achieving your dreams may be long and winding, but with a strong foundation of motivation, a clear understanding of your goals, and the right strategies in place, there is no limit to what you can achieve. Carry forward the lessons and insights you've gained, and let them light your way as you continue on your journey toward success and fulfillment.

In the end, the true essence of motivation lies in its ability to transform not just our actions but our very lives. By harnessing this powerful force, you open the door to a world of possibilities where your dreams and aspirations are not just distant wishes but achievable realities. So, as you step forward from here, do so with confidence, determination, and an unwavering commitment to your journey of continuous growth and achievement.

Chapter Three

Setting Epic Goals

At the heart of every achievement lies a goal, a light that guides you through the uncertain times of life toward success. Goals are not just milestones—they are the very essence of motivation, providing a clear and tangible roadmap to realizing our dreams. They are the foundation upon which you build your aspirations, the first and most crucial step in the journey of achievement.

The Transformative Impact of Goals

Research, both in clinical settings and in real-life experiences, has repeatedly shown that goals are instrumental in accelerating success and personal growth. Setting goals allows you to take stock of your current position in your personal and professional lives and serves as a catalyst to craft the future you envision. It's about living with intention, shaping your destiny, and ensuring that life happens for you, not to you.

Understanding Goal-Setting Theory

The concept of goal setting was revolutionized by Edwin Locke, whose seminal study "Toward a Theory of Task Motivation and Incentives" in 1968 laid the groundwork for what would become known as goal setting theory. Locke's research was further expanded upon to provide more concrete advice on setting and achieving goals.

This theory underscores a vital insight: having a clear, conscious, and purposeful goal significantly increases the likelihood of realizing your desires. It highlights the importance of knowing precisely what you want and devising a strategic plan to make progress toward these aims.

The Role of Motivation in Goal Achievement

T. A. Ryan, in the paper "Intentional Behavior" (1970), posited that motivation is what differentiates the successful from the rest, assuming equal capabilities. Since personal goals are a proven way to foster motivation, they play a pivotal role in driving success. Goals ignite your inner drive, focusing your energy and resources on results.

Strategies for Effective Goal Setting

So, what are the proven strategies for setting goals that lead to success? The core principles of goal-setting theory provide a framework for this. These include setting clear, measurable, and achievable goals, ensuring they are challenging yet realistic, creating short-term milestones for long-term objectives, and continuously monitoring and adjusting your approach based on progress and feedback.

Five Principles of Goal Setting Theory

Psychologists Edwin Locke and Gary Latham's goal-setting theory illuminates the path to success through five key principles. These principles act as a compass, guiding you toward effectively setting and achieving your goals, both in your professional and personal life.

Clarity: The Power of Precision

The first principle, clarity, emphasizes the importance of setting goals that are clear and specific. Vague goals are like trying to hit a target in the fog, but clear goals bring the target into sharp focus. For instance, rather than aiming to "increase sales," a more precise goal would be to "increase sales by 10% in the next quarter." This principle advocates for goals that are well-defined and include a specific timeframe, ensuring that you can measure your progress and know exactly when you've achieved your objective.

Challenge: Balancing Aspiration with Attainability

Challenging goals stir the spirit and inspire greater effort and perseverance. However, the key is to strike a balance between ambition and realism. Goals should stretch your abilities but remain attainable. The joy of achieving a challenging goal fuels your journey toward subsequent objectives. While setting these goals, ensure they are not so lofty that they become demotivating due to their unattainability.

Commitment: Following Through with Motivation

Commitment to your goals is essential for success. It's about having a genuine desire and taking ownership of your objectives. This commitment involves a dedication to the process and an openness to the growth and learning that comes from pursuing these goals. Without this sense of commitment and self-regulation, the motivation to work toward your goals diminishes.

Feedback: The Catalyst for Adjustment and Growth

Regular feedback is crucial in navigating the journey toward your goals. This feedback, whether self-assessed or from others, provides valuable insights into your progress. It enables you to adjust your strategies and refine your goals, ensuring they remain aligned with your aspirations and capacities. Embrace feedback as a tool for continuous improvement and realignment toward your success.

Task Complexity: Managing Intricacy with Strategy

For complex goals, understanding and acknowledging their intricacy is vital. Break down these larger goals into smaller, manageable tasks. This breakdown makes the process less overwhelming and provides a clearer pathway to achievement. For instance, writing an article could be divided into stages like choosing a topic, researching sources, drafting, inserting SEO keywords, and revising. Each stage can then be tackled systematically.

Applying Goal Setting Theory: A Practical Example

To bring these principles to life, let's consider a practical example. Suppose your goal is to enhance your professional skills in digital marketing. In this case, applying the five principles would look like this:

- Clarity: Enroll in a certified digital marketing course by the end of the month.

- Challenge: Choose a course that is recognized for its rigor and comprehensive content.

- Commitment: Dedicate specific hours each week to study and practice the skills learned.

- Feedback: Regularly assess your progress through assignments and seek feedback from instructors or peers.

- Task Complexity: Break down the learning process into modules like SEO, content marketing, and social media marketing, and approach each module systematically.

The Significance of Goal Setting in Your Life

Goal setting is a critical component of success and satisfaction, offering numerous advantages that underscore its importance. Here are six compelling reasons to embrace goal setting and consistently strive for goal attainment.

Focus and Direction

Without a goal, efforts can scatter like leaves in the wind, lacking direction and purpose. Setting a goal is akin to focusing the flight of a hummingbird to the precision of a hawk descending upon its target. It sharpens your daily focus, allowing you to concentrate your efforts effectively, minimizing wasted energy and aimless actions.

Tracking Progress and Growth

The ability to track progress is only possible with defined goals. Monitoring advancements toward these goals can be immensely satisfying, fueling your motivation and resilience. It also enables the application of preventive psychology, helping you to stave off discouragement by recognizing the incremental progress you've made. Understanding that you're moving forward, albeit gradually, is a powerful antidote to the sense of being stagnant.

Sustained Motivation

Goals are the engines of motivation, propelling you to make sh** happen even on days when inaction seems compelling. Consider the dedication of an athlete with a competition in sight—their goal compels them to train relentlessly, overcoming fatigue, discomfort, and reluctance. Similarly, a clear goal provides you with intrinsic motivation, keeping you engaged and driving toward higher performance.

Overcoming Procrastination

Goals are a formidable weapon against the lure of procrastination. Recognizing the value of each day and the incremental progress toward your goals underscores the peril of delay. Fred Brook's profound words, "How does a project get to be a year late?...One day at a time," poignantly highlight the urgency and importance of action in the pursuit of your objectives.

Achieving and Surpassing Expectations

Achieving a goal is a taste of victory that often fuels the desire for further success. Goal setting cultivates a habit of pushing your limits, challenging yourself to scale new heights, and achieving more than you previously thought possible. This process of continuous improvement and goal attainment leads to accomplishments beyond your initial expectations.

Clarifying Life Aspirations

Setting goals necessitates introspection and contemplation about what you truly desire in life. It prompts questions about your ideal level of success, desired income, lifestyle aspirations, and long-term dreams. Through this process, you break down these overarching desires into tangible, attainable goals, which then act as stepping-stones toward your ultimate aspirations.

Common Goal-Setting Pitfalls

Setting Unwritten Goals

Goals that aren't written down have about as much substance as a ghost—they're there but not quite. Writing down your goals is like giving them a body, a presence. It turns a wishful thought into a tangible action plan. Remember, an unwritten goal is just a daydream with ambition.

The Rabbit Chase Conundrum

As the old proverb warns, chasing too many rabbits often leads to a dinner of leaves and twigs. While having a plethora of goals sounds ambitious, it often results in catching none. Aim for a sweet spot—not too few that you're lounging in comfort, but not so many that you're in a perpetual state of rabbit-chasing frenzy.

The One-Trick Pony Syndrome

Focusing solely on career goals is like eating only potatoes every day—it's nourishing but bland. Life is a smorgasbord of experiences. Set goals in various life areas—personal, relational, spiritual, physical—to enjoy a well-rounded and flavorful existence.

Setting Vague Goals

Setting vague goals is like trying to catch fog in a net—it's an exercise in futility. Be specific. Instead of saying, "I want to write a book," declare,

"I will write a 300-page sci-fi novel by December." Precision is the soul of progress.

Setting Immeasurable Goals

Goals without measurable outcomes are like scales that don't show numbers—they leave you guessing. "Lose weight" is as clear as mud. "Lose ten pounds by April"—now that's a goal with clarity. When in doubt, throw in a number or a percentage.

The Deadline Dilemma

A goal without a deadline is like a ship without a rudder—directionless and destined to float aimlessly. Deadlines inject a sense of urgency and help prioritize your actions. Remember, "someday" is not a day in the week.

The Out of Sight, Out of Mind Trap

Writing goals and then forgetting about them is like planting seeds and never watering them—nothing grows. Keep your goals where you can see them, whether it's a daily review or a weekly check-in. Out of sight, out of mind; in sight, in line.

The Comfort Zone Cozy-Up

Setting goals that don't stretch you is like jogging on a treadmill—you're moving but not really going anywhere. Step out of your comfort zone. Your goals should make you a tad nervous and excited, like the first day of school.

Setting Goals without Motivation

Goals without personal significance are like rockets without fuel—they won't launch. Write down why each goal matters to you. This is the emotional rocket fuel that will propel you through the "messy middle" of your journey.

The Action Plan Delay

Overplanning your goals can be an elegant form of procrastination. Identify the next immediate action—that's your starting point. Remember, you don't have to see the whole staircase, just the first step.

As we step into the future, remember that the coming year can be a rerun or a revelation, an echo, or an adventure. The choice is yours. Set your goals wisely, avoid these common pitfalls, and you might just find yourself in a story worth telling.

Setting Achievable Goals for Sustained Success

The art of setting achievable goals is a cornerstone of success and personal fulfillment. Properly established goals not only propel you toward your dreams but also safeguard you against the disheartening effects of unmet objectives. Let's explore how to craft goals that are not just aspirational but attainable, ensuring a journey of continued motivation and growth.

Harmonize your Goals with Personal Values

The most resonant and achievable goals are those that align with your core values. Like a compass guiding a ship, your values steer your actions and decisions. Before embarking on goal setting, conduct a thorough inventory of your values. Understanding what truly matters to you will illuminate the path to setting meaningful and attainable goals.

For instance, if your value is prioritizing comfort over health, a goal to lose weight might feel more burdensome than inspiring. Recognizing and realigning your goals to match your values is a crucial step in ensuring they are not only set but met.

Lawyer and motivational writer Robin Sharma eloquently said, "The real value of setting and achieving goals lies not in the rewards you receive but in the person you become as a result of reaching your goals."

Embracing Simplicity and Focus

When it comes to goal setting, less is often more. Focusing on one or two primary goals at a time prevents the pitfall of "goal competition," where too many objectives dilute your focus and energy. Start by identifying your most critical goals, then break these down into smaller, manageable steps. This approach facilitates ongoing, incremental changes, which are more sustainable than attempting to overhaul everything simultaneously.

Set SMART Goals

The SMART framework, developed by Edwin Locke and Gary Latham, provides a structured approach to setting effective goals. The acronym SMART stands for Specific, Measurable, Achievable, Relevant, and Time-Bound, encompassing the five essential characteristics of effective goal setting.

- Specific: Clearly define the goal and the actions required to achieve it.

- Measurable: Determine the metrics or indicators of progress.

- Achievable: Ensure the goal is realistic, considering available resources and skills.

- Relevant: Align the goal with your broader objectives, values, and life purpose.

- Time-Bound: Set a definitive timeline for completion, breaking the goal into smaller milestones with their own deadlines.

SMART goals embody the balance between challenge and realism, making them ambitious yet within reach. By setting specific, challenging goals with a target completion date, you significantly enhance your chances of success.

Cultivate an Environment Conducive to Achieve Your Goals

Creating an environment that supports your goals is as crucial as setting the goals themselves. Often, your surroundings influence your actions more than you realize. By aligning your physical and social environment with your aspirations, you set the stage for success and make the journey toward your goals smoother and more attainable.

Minimizing Distractions and Temptations

Just as a gardener removes weeds to allow the plants to thrive, removing distractions from your environment can significantly boost your focus and productivity. For example, keeping your phone out of arm's reach can prevent late-night social media browsing that cuts into your sleep. Or, ridding your kitchen of junk food can be a game-changer if you're striving for healthier eating habits. By eliminating these environmental temptations, you align your daily habits with your goals.

Organization and Preparation

The principle of "choice architecture," as demonstrated in Anne Thorndike's nutrition research, shows that the way you organize your environment can significantly impact your decisions and behaviors. For instance, laying out your gym clothes the night before simplifies your morning routine, making it easier to fit in the workout. Similarly, keeping noise-canceling headphones handy can improve concentration in noisy settings. Small acts of organization and preparation can make a big difference in achieving your goals.

Create a Vision Board

A vision board can be a powerful tool in goal setting. Neuroscientist Tara Swart, in her book *The Source: The Secrets of the Universe, The Science of the Brain*, discusses how vision boards prime our brains to recognize and seize opportunities. Since our brains give more weight to images than words, a vision board complements a written list of goals, keeping your aspirations visually and mentally in focus.

Surrounding Yourself with Positivity

The company you keep and the media you consume can greatly influence your mindset and motivation. Engage with people and content that uplift and inspire you. Choose to absorb positive images, music, books, and stories that reinforce the pursuit of your goals, helping to keep your spirits high and your focus sharp.

Daily Goal Analysis

Consistently reviewing and assessing your goals is key to maintaining progress. This daily analysis involves evaluating the tasks completed, the realistic nature of your goals, and how your daily actions align with your long-term objectives. It's a process of self-reflection and adjustment, ensuring that your goals remain relevant and attainable.

Remember, as baseball legend Steve Garvey said, "You have to set goals that are almost out of reach." If your goals don't stretch you, they won't challenge you to reach your full potential. Aim high, but ensure your goals are grounded in your capabilities and environment.

Conclusion

As you conclude this chapter on goal setting, it's essential to reflect on the journey you've embarked upon. Setting goals is not merely a task to be checked off—it's a transformative process that shapes your life, your behaviors, and, ultimately, your destiny. Throughout this chapter, you've navigated the nuances of effective goal setting, uncovering strategies to make your aspirations not only reachable but also meaningful.

You've learned the importance of setting clear, specific, and measurable goals that challenge you yet remain within the realm of achievability. You've delved into the significance of aligning your goals with your personal values, ensuring that your pursuits resonate deeply with who you are and what you stand for. You've seen how creating a supportive environment, both physically and socially, can significantly enhance your ability to meet your objectives. And you've understood the critical role of regular reflection and adjustment in keeping your goals relevant and your motivation strong.

Goal setting is an art and a science. It requires a careful balance of ambition and realism, of dreaming big while staying grounded in actionable steps. It's about understanding that while goals are destinations, the journey toward them is equally important. This journey is filled with learning, growth, and self-discovery. It's about becoming the best version of yourself, one goal at a time.

As you move forward, carry with you the lessons learned and the strategies discussed. Approach your goals with a renewed sense of purpose and a clear vision. Remember, the goals you set today are the stepping-stones to the life you aspire to live tomorrow. They are the blueprints of your future, the framework upon which you build your dreams.

Chapter Four

Overcoming Procrastination with Laughs

Ah, procrastination—that all-too-familiar term for delay and distractions, where to-do lists languish and intentions tumble into the feeling of "later." If you find yourself drawn to cat videos, the call of online shopping, or the act of space-staring when you should be making sh** happen, then you're familiar with procrastination.

Procrastination is the art of postponing decisions or actions without justifiable cause. It's like knowing you have a marathon to run but choosing to tie your shoelaces only when you hear the starting gun. For instance, a student procrastinating studying for an exam until the eve of the test, despite knowing that an earlier start would be wiser, is a textbook example.

Procrastination isn't a modern-day phenomenon. It has left its footprints across history, with many famous personalities being notorious procrastinators. Instead of writing The *Hunchback of Notre Dame*, renowned author Victor Hugo spent an entire year throwing parties, starting other projects, and ignoring his manuscript. Despite getting a promotion that let him leave work in the early afternoon, writer Franz

Kafka often didn't begin putting pen to paper until eleven o'clock at night. Prodigal composer Amadeus Mozart wrote Don Giovanni the night before the performance, leaving the musicians no time for practice. And even Frank Lloyd Wright's architectural masterpieces often sprang from last-minute efforts. So the next time you find yourself face to face with procrastination, remember that you aren't alone. But keep in mind that while sitting on the couch watching your favorite TV show for the tenth time might be the safe option, your Don Giovanni will never be heard, your Metamorphosis never read, and your architectural legend never built until you make sh** happen.

Psychologists' View of Procrastination

Did you know that around 20% of adults in the U.S. are what you'd call chronic procrastinators? This fact, highlighted by Joseph Ferrari, a psychology professor at DePaul University and the author of *Still Procrastinating: The No-Regret Guide to Getting It Done*, underscores just how common procrastination is. It's not just a quirky habit but a widespread phenomenon.

No matter how organized or dedicated you might be, there's a good chance you've caught yourself wasting hours on seemingly minor activities (like binge-watching TV shows, endlessly scrolling through social media, or indulging in online shopping) when you really should have been working on important tasks.

Procrastination is not picky; it can creep into various aspects of life. Be it delaying a crucial work project, avoiding school assignments, or ignoring household chores, procrastination can significantly impact your professional life, academic performance, and overall daily living.

Types of Procrastinators

Procrastination, a familiar foe to many, comes in various forms. Understanding these can be the key to unlocking more effective ways of managing time and tasks. Researchers have identified several types of procrastination, each with its unique characteristics.

Passive vs. Active Procrastinators

Passive Procrastinators: These individuals delay tasks due to indecision. They're not intentionally putting off tasks; they're simply struggling to make decisions and act on them. Imagine someone wanting to start a diet but can't decide which one, resulting in no diet at all.

Active Procrastinators: In contrast, active procrastinators are the adrenaline junkies of task management. They delay tasks on purpose, thriving under the pressure of looming deadlines. They find that the rush of a time crunch is what really gets their gears turning.

Behavioral Styles of Procrastination

- **The Perfectionists:** Afraid of falling short of perfection, they hesitate to start or finish tasks.

- **The Dreamers:** Not fans of the nitty-gritty details, these procrastinators often find themselves lost in the bigger picture without a clear path to action.

- **The Defiers:** These types dislike external control over their schedule. They may procrastinate as a form of rebellion against imposed timelines or tasks.

- **The Worriers:** Change is the enemy of worriers. They prefer the comfort of the known and delay tasks that might put them in new, unfamiliar situations.

- **The Crisis-Makers:** These procrastinators love the drama of the eleventh-hour scramble. They believe they thrive when the pressure is on.

- **The Overdoers:** Taking on too much, overdoers find themselves swamped, leading to the inability to start or complete tasks.

Procrastinators vs. Non-Procrastinators

According to international researcher, writer, and psychologist Dr. Joseph Ferrari, non-procrastinators focus squarely on the task at hand. They possess a strong sense of personal identity and are less concerned with social esteem—the regard of others—as opposed to their own self-esteem. Psychologist Piers Steel notes that people who don't procrastinate tend to rank high in conscientiousness, a trait associated with self-discipline, persistence, and personal responsibility. This trait is part of the Big Five personality theory, a widely recognized model in psychology.

The Negative Impact of Procrastination

Procrastination is often seen as a harmless habit, but its impact goes far beyond delaying tasks. It's a phenomenon that can affect not only your productivity and happiness but also your mental and physical health. The effects of procrastination are subtle yet deeply consequential, shaping your beliefs, opportunities, goals, career, and self-esteem.

Fostering Limiting Beliefs

Continuous procrastination can lead to the formation of limiting beliefs about your capabilities and potential. These beliefs gradually solidify into a negative self-identity, fostering a cycle of more procrastination and self-doubt. This cycle can trigger a downward spiral, where you increasingly view yourself as a failure, doubt your abilities, and miss out on realizing your full potential.

Managing emotions effectively is crucial in breaking this cycle. It's about learning to overcome these limiting beliefs and embracing a more positive and realistic view of your abilities and possibilities.

Missing Life-Changing Opportunities

Think about the times you've missed out on crucial opportunities due to procrastination. These missed chances could have been transformative, but the habit of delaying decisions or actions meant that the opportunity slipped through your fingers. Whether it's a last-minute rush on a crucial project or hesitating to seize a new venture, procrastination can cost you dearly in terms of growth and success.

Life's opportunities are precious and often fleeting. Embracing them when they arise is essential for personal and professional development.

Derailing Goals

Procrastination becomes particularly potent when it comes to pursuing goals. You might have a burning desire to achieve something, but procrastination keeps you from taking the first step. This paradoxical situation—where you want to achieve but don't act—is often a source of confusion and frustration.

Understanding and addressing the underlying reasons for this resistance is key. If not dealt with, procrastination can significantly diminish your chances of improving your life through your goals.

Jeopardizing Career

In a professional context, procrastination can be especially damaging. It affects how much you accomplish and the quality of your performance. Habitual procrastination may lead to missed deadlines, unmet targets, and a negative reputation at work, potentially affecting promotions and job security. The consequences of long-term procrastination in a work environment can be career-limiting or even career-ending.

Eroding Self-Esteem

Procrastination and self-esteem can be locked in a harmful cycle. Low self-esteem can lead to procrastination, as you might doubt your ability to complete tasks effectively. In turn, procrastination can exacerbate feelings of low self-esteem, creating a vicious circle. Research involving college students has shown that procrastination is negatively associated with self-esteem and self-control.

Impairing Decision-Making

One of the more insidious effects of procrastination is its impact on decision-making. When you procrastinate, your choices are often dictated by the pressure of dwindling time or the anxiety of looming deadlines. Decisions made in haste can lead to unfavorable outcomes, as they are influenced more by fear and stress rather than rational thinking.

To mitigate this, try to find a moment of calm to thoughtfully weigh the pros and cons of each option. Even if procrastination has already set in, taking a step back to carefully consider your choices can help make more balanced and beneficial decisions moving forward.

Damaging Reputation

Consistently failing to follow through on commitments can tarnish your reputation. Over time, people may begin to perceive you as unreliable, which can affect both professional and personal relationships. This repeated behavior can also erode your self-esteem and self-confidence, making it even easier to fall into the trap of procrastination.

However, it's never too late to change. Start by meeting small commitments and gradually take on bigger tasks. With each fulfilled promise, you'll start to rebuild trust and improve your image.

Endangering Mental Health

Chronic procrastination can lead to increased stress and anxiety, particularly when it affects others or important projects. This constant state of stress can contribute to mental health issues like depression, creating a vicious cycle where the more depressed you feel, the harder it becomes to take action.

Addressing the root causes of your procrastination is essential. Rather than just putting off tasks, understand that procrastinating can mean choosing a path of increased stress and potential mental health challenges.

Affecting Physical Health

Neglecting to take care of your physical health is another consequence of procrastination. Delaying exercise, regular check-ups, or even simple self-care routines can have serious implications for your physical well-being.

Research has linked chronic procrastination with health problems like insomnia, headaches, and even cardiovascular diseases. The delayed approach to health can exacerbate problems, making them more difficult to manage later on.

Losing Precious Time

Perhaps the most apparent yet overlooked impact of procrastination is the loss of time. The hours, days, or even years spent delaying tasks and goals accumulate, leading to a significant portion of life spent in inaction. The realization that time has passed without much change can be a sobering and often regretful experience.

Strategies for Overcoming Procrastination

Dealing with procrastination can be a challenging task, but there are effective strategies that can help you overcome it. By understanding the root cause of your procrastination and adopting practical approaches, you can start tackling tasks more efficiently and reduce the habit of delaying important work.

Identify the Reason for Procrastination

Whenever you catch yourself procrastinating, pause and reflect: "Why am I delaying this task?" Understanding the reason behind your procrastination is crucial. It could be due to fear, uncertainty, boredom, or overwhelming complexity. Identifying the cause allows you to address it more effectively.

Break Down Tasks into Manageable Steps

Large or complex tasks can be intimidating, leading to procrastination. Break these tasks into smaller, manageable steps. This approach makes a daunting project more approachable, similar to climbing a series of small hills instead of a single mountain.

For individuals with ADHD, who might struggle with visualizing the entire project, getting assistance in organizing tasks can be helpful. However, be wary of falling into the trap of overplanning, where the planning stage itself becomes a form of procrastination.

Set Deadlines for Smaller Goals

Once you have broken down the task, set specific deadlines for each smaller goal. This method transforms a distant and overwhelming target into a series of short-term, achievable objectives. Celebrate each small victory with a reward, shifting away from last-minute rushes and fostering a sense of continuous progress.

Leverage Positive Social Pressure

An accountability partner can provide the necessary motivation to start and continue a project. Commit your goals and timelines to a friend or colleague. This social commitment can create a gentle but effective push toward action.

Collaborating with someone on a task can also maintain engagement and momentum, especially for tasks that feel mundane or tedious.

Make Tedious Tasks Interesting

If boredom is causing you to procrastinate, find ways to make the task more engaging. Challenge yourself to complete a certain amount of work within a time limit, listen to music to make the activity more enjoyable, or set up a reward for when the task is completed. These strategies can transform a dull task into a more stimulating experience.

Rotate Between Tasks

If your interest wanes easily, try alternating between two different tasks. This can keep your engagement levels high and prevent boredom. Use a timer to dedicate equal intervals to each task, ensuring that you make progress on both fronts.

Commit to Short Work Bursts

Starting a task can sometimes be the hardest part. Commit to working on it for just ten minutes. Often, those first few minutes are enough to break through the barrier of resistance. If you're still finding it hard to continue after ten minutes, take a short break and then commit to another ten-minute block.

Minimize Distractions

Eliminate external and internal distractions as much as possible. Turn off your phone, close unnecessary browser tabs, and create a work environment conducive to focus. Beware of 'busy work' that feels productive but actually distracts you from the main task.

Delegate Tasks Wisely

Recognize when it's more effective to delegate tasks to someone else. While learning new skills is beneficial, sometimes it's more efficient to rely on others' expertise. For instance, you don't need to become a mechanic to fix your car—that's what professional mechanics are for. Understand that delegating is not a sign of weakness or incompetence; it's a strategic choice that can save time and reduce stress.

Replace Negative Thoughts with Positive Reinforcement

The power of our thoughts in shaping our actions cannot be overstated. Engaging in positive self-talk and reminding yourself of your successes can motivate you to start and continue tasks. In contrast, negative thoughts can deepen the cycle of avoidance and procrastination.

Use CBT as a Tool Against Procrastination

If negative thinking is a significant factor in your procrastination, consider cognitive behavioral therapy (CBT). Research has shown that CBT can be a valuable tool in combating procrastination. In studies where participants with severe procrastination underwent CBT, either through self-guided online programs or in group settings, significant improvements were observed. Participants not only reduced their procrastination but also experienced betterment in related areas like anxiety, depression, and overall well-being.

Conclusion

As you conclude this chapter on procrastination, you come to understand that it is more than just a simple habit of delaying tasks.

It's a complex behavior based on your emotions, thought processes, and life circumstances. Throughout this chapter, you've learned that procrastination can stem from a range of factors, including fear of failure or lack of motivation. By recognizing the specific reasons behind our procrastination, you can tailor your approach to managing it more effectively.

You've also discovered that there are practical and psychological strategies to combat procrastination. Breaking tasks into smaller, manageable parts, setting deadlines, and rewarding yourself for completing these tasks can help you maintain motivation and progress. At the same time, understanding the importance of delegation and the power of positive thinking can significantly impact your ability to tackle tasks promptly.

Keep in mind the role of CBT in addressing the negative thought patterns that often fuel procrastination. By reshaping your thinking, you can break the cycle of delay and avoidance, paving the way for more productive and fulfilling actions.

In summary, procrastination is a complex issue that requires practical solutions. Whether it's through practical task management, psychological interventions, or a combination of both, you have the power to overcome the grip of procrastination. By applying the insights and strategies discussed in this chapter, you can turn procrastination from a persistent obstacle into a conquered challenge, opening the door to enhanced productivity, improved mental health, and a greater sense of accomplishment in your daily life.

Chapter Five

Hacking Productivity with a Sense of Humor

Time management is a vital skill that involves strategically organizing and allocating your time across various activities. It's about finding an efficient way to use your time so that you can accomplish what you need to do without feeling overwhelmed or stressed. With effective time management, you can identify and prioritize tasks based on their urgency and importance, focusing your efforts on what truly matters.

The Essence of Time Management

Good time management enables you to work smarter, not harder. It's about making the most of your available time and using it to focus on the tasks that have the greatest impact. It involves planning your days and weeks in a way that balances high-priority work with less urgent tasks, ensuring that everything gets the attention it needs without last-minute rushes or burnout.

Understanding Productivity

Productivity is often misunderstood as simply doing more things within a given timeframe. However, true productivity is about completing important tasks consistently. It's not about speeding through a long to-do list but rather maintaining a steady pace on key tasks. Productivity is measured by the efficiency and effectiveness with which you complete these tasks. This approach ensures that you're not just busy but genuinely productive.

Improve Your Time Management and Productivity Skills

"I have two kinds of problems, the urgent and the important. The urgent are not important, and the important and never urgent." These are the words former President Dwight D. Eisenhower said in a 1954 speech. Unknowingly, that day, he did more than inspire a school of university students; he also created the idea that would turn into the Eisenhower Matrix. The Eisenhower Matrix is a way to become more productive by prioritizing tasks by placing them into two categories: urgent and important. To further enhance your time management skills and practice the Eisenhower Matrix, consider the following strategies:

Set Clear Goals: Define what you want to achieve in a specific period—be it a day, a week, or a month. Clear goals give you direction and a benchmark to measure your progress.

Prioritize Tasks: Not all tasks are created equal. Identify which tasks are urgent and important and tackle them first. Less critical tasks can be scheduled for later.

Use Tools and Techniques: Leverage tools like calendars, planners, and apps to organize your tasks. Techniques like the Pomodoro Technique or time-blocking can also help you manage your time more effectively.

Avoid Multitasking: Focus on one task at a time. Multitasking often leads to lower-quality work and decreased productivity.

Take Breaks: Regular breaks are essential. They help maintain your energy levels and keep your mind fresh.

Productivity and Its Myths

Productivity isn't about constantly working or filling your day with tasks. It's about making meaningful progress in the areas that matter most. It's okay to have downtime and to say no to tasks that don't align with your goals. Remember, being constantly busy doesn't equate to being effective.

Unraveling the Productivity Trap

The productivity trap is a paradoxical situation where increased efficiency in work leads not to more leisure time but to an ever-expanding workload. This trap is a cycle of continuously adding more tasks as you become more efficient, resulting in increased stress and anxiety due to the perception of an impossible volume of work.

Understanding the Productivity Trap

Imagine you've just finished your tasks efficiently and now have some free time. Instead of taking a well-deserved break, you pile on more tasks. This increase in workload doesn't come with an increase in energy or resources needed to handle it. Over time, this leads to burnout, stress, and a sense of perpetual inadequacy.

The Never-Ending Task List

Imagine finishing your work early, with visions of your favorite Netflix show dancing in your head. But then, like a sneaky ninja, more tasks appear out of nowhere. It's like playing a game of whack-a-mole—for every task you knock down, two more pop up. You start to wonder if your task list is breeding overnight.

The Industrial Revolution Hangover

Journalist and author Oliver Burkeman points out that the productivity trap started with the industrial revolution. It's as if factories were the first to say, "Great job! Now, do it twice as fast!" People went from "early to bed, early to rise" to "you can sleep when you're dead" in a matter of decades. Now, they're like hamsters on a wheel, running faster and getting nowhere.

Digital Age Dilemmas

Enter the digital age, where technology was supposed to make life easier. Instead, you're drowning in a sea of productivity apps that promise to streamline our lives. It's like having a personal trainer for every aspect of your day. But instead of getting fitter, you're just getting busier. You start to miss the days when a "sync" was just something in your kitchen.

The Hedonic Treadmill

The hedonic adaptation or hedonic treadmill is kind of like opening presents at Christmas. You make a list, you check it twice, and as the day gets nearer and nearer, your anticipation begins to grow. Finally, it's time. You rip through your gifts in a flurry of wrapping paper, filled with joy and happiness at the things you have. But that spike of happiness slowly begins to recede, leaving you in your normal state of contentment. The hedonic treadmill argues that every person has a set happiness point. No matter what we go through or how hard we might try to become happier, we'll always come back to the same place. It's like chasing a rainbow—you can run as fast and far as you want, but you'll never quite get to the pot of gold.

Breaking Free

To escape the productivity trap, it's important to sometimes play the role of a rebellious teenager. Set boundaries with your work like it's a 10 PM curfew. Embrace the art of doing nothing—it's not being lazy; it's a strategic recharge. Remember, every time you say "no" to extra work, an overworked employee gets their wings.

Quality over Quantity

Instead of trying to juggle a hundred balls and dropping fifty, juggle ten and put on a great show. It's better to be a master of a few trades than a frazzled jack-of-all. Focus on doing a few things well rather than doing everything with the finesse of a sleepy sloth.

Strategies for Enhancing Productivity

Maximizing productivity is an essential skill in the fast-paced world you live in. By adopting effective productivity hacks, you can ensure that each day is spent efficiently, making the most of your time and energy. Here are some key strategies to enhance your daily productivity:

Plan Your Day in Advance

Organizing your day beforehand is crucial. A clear plan provides direction and helps prioritize tasks. Either the night before or early in the morning, outline your schedule, detailing what needs to be done and when. This planning eliminates guesswork and reduces the likelihood of time wasted on indecision.

Identify Three Key Tasks Daily

Each day, identify the three most important tasks and describe them in detail. Focusing on these key tasks ensures that your efforts are concentrated on the most impactful activities rather than just the most urgent ones.

Adopt a Productivity Technique

Incorporate a productivity technique that resonates with you. Try the Pomodoro Technique. Set a timer and work on a singular task. When the timer is up, take a short break and then move on to the next Pomodoro task. Or try the Eisenhower Matrix or another system. Find a method that helps you stay focused and organize your day around achievable goals.

Set a Single Daily Goal

Aim to have one primary goal for each day. This approach allows you to devote your full attention to one major task at a time. Break down this goal into smaller tasks if necessary, allocating specific times to focus solely on them.

Designate Specific Times for Checking Emails

Limit the time spent on checking emails, as it can be a significant distraction. Schedule specific times for this—perhaps once before lunch and again at the end of the workday—to avoid constant interruptions.

Learn to Say "No"

Develop the ability to decline requests or tasks that do not align with your priorities. Saying no is essential for maintaining focus on your goals and managing your time effectively.

Utilize Website Blockers

To minimize distractions, especially from online sources, use website blockers. These tools can prevent you from accessing websites that interrupt your workflow.

Optimize Your Workspace with Red and Blue

Enhance your workspace with red and blue colors. Research suggests that these colors can boost brain performance: red helps with attention to detail while blue encourages creativity. Organizing and decluttering your desk also aids in maintaining a focused and productive work environment.

Use Two-Minute Rule for Small Tasks

Don't let indecision about small tasks interrupt your flow. Apply the two-minute rule: if a task can be completed in two minutes or less, do it immediately. Otherwise, add it to your to-do list. This approach keeps minor tasks from accumulating and becoming overwhelming.

Listen to Music that Enhances Your Focus

Music can be a powerful tool for maintaining focus and enhancing productivity. Choose tunes that help you concentrate. Instrumental music or specific "focus" playlists can be particularly effective.

Make Templates for Routine Tasks

For tasks you perform regularly, create templates. This streamlines your process, saving time and effort, allowing you to focus on more complex tasks.

Group Similar Tasks

Group similar tasks together and complete them in one go. This batching technique ensures you stay in the same mental zone, enhancing efficiency and making your workflow smoother.

Avoid Multitasking

Multitasking is often less effective than focusing on one task at a time. Research indicates that multitasking can significantly reduce productivity. Focus on single tasks to improve quality and efficiency.

Use the Important/Urgent Matrix

Implement the Eisenhower Matrix (Important/Urgent Matrix) to prioritize tasks. This method helps categorize tasks based on urgency and importance, ensuring you focus on what truly matters.

Start Your Day Strategically

Begin your day with either the toughest task to get it out of the way or an easy task to build momentum. This sets the tone for a productive day.

"One and Done" Rule

When a new task arises, immediately add it to your to-do list. This prevents tasks from being forgotten or endlessly postponed.

Take Effective Breaks

Regular breaks are crucial for maintaining focus and productivity. Use breaks to fully disengage from work, whether through meditation or simply relaxing, to recharge effectively.

Plan Your Breaks

Create a break agenda with activities you enjoy. This ensures your breaks are refreshing and that you return to work rejuvenated.

Work in Short Bursts

Use techniques like the Pomodoro method, working in focused bursts with short breaks in between. This keeps your mind sharp and motivated.

Dedicated Workspace

Establish a specific area for work, especially if you're remote or home-based. This helps create a boundary between work and personal life.

Utilize Natural Light

Set up your workspace near a source of natural light. Sunlight boosts mood and energy, enhancing your productivity.

Eliminate Distractions

Identify and eliminate potential distractions. This could mean turning off notifications, using website blockers, or creating a quiet work environment.

Break Down Large Goals

Divide big goals into smaller, achievable steps. This makes them more manageable and less daunting, fitting more easily into your daily or weekly plans.

Begin Work Mindfully Each Morning

Begin each day with a few minutes of reflection on your work. Think about the previous day's achievements or set clear intentions for the day ahead. This practice helps transition your mind from rest mode to work mode, establishing a purposeful mindset for the day.

Embrace the Power of Early Mornings

Waking up early can provide a quiet, distraction-free environment that's ideal for productivity. The calm of the early morning hours often leads to enhanced focus and efficiency, allowing you to tackle important tasks with renewed energy.

Align Tasks with Long-Term Goals

Before embarking on a task, assess its relevance to your long-term objectives, such as those defined in your SMART goals. If a task doesn't contribute to your broader goals, consider delegating it or removing it from your list. This ensures that your efforts are consistently aligned with your larger aspirations.

Adhere to Deadlines

Set and follow deadlines, even if you have a generous timeframe for a task. A sense of urgency fostered by deadlines can enhance focus and efficiency, helping you complete tasks in a timely manner.

Prioritize Self-Care

Regularly schedule time for self-care activities to prevent burnout. Whether it's reading, walking, meditating, or pursuing a hobby, these activities are crucial for recharging your mental and physical energy.

Don't Be a Perfectionist

Acknowledge that perfection is an unattainable standard. Striving for excellence is commendable, but getting bogged down by perfectionism can hinder progress. Learn to recognize when work is "good enough" and move forward.

Find Your Motivation

Reflect on the reasons why you chose your profession or field of work. Keeping these motivations in mind can provide a constant source of inspiration and drive, helping you stay engaged and productive.

Leverage Technology Wisely

Use technology to enhance productivity, but be mindful of its potential to distract. Choose apps and tools that streamline your workflow and avoid digital platforms that lead to time-wasting.

Regularly Review and Adjust Goals

Periodically review your long-term goals and the progress you've made toward them. This not only keeps you on track but also allows you to adjust your strategies and priorities as needed.

Cultivate a Growth Mindset

Adopt a mindset that embraces challenges and views failures as opportunities for learning and growth. This approach encourages continuous self-improvement and resilience.

By implementing these advanced productivity techniques, you can significantly improve your ability to manage time and tasks. These strategies are designed to enhance focus, streamline workflow, and ensure that you're not just busy but effectively and efficiently working toward your goals. You can significantly improve your daily productivity. Effective time management, focusing on key tasks, and creating an optimal work environment are all crucial steps in becoming more productive. Remember, productivity is not just about doing more—it's about doing what is important efficiently and effectively.

Conclusion

Productivity encompasses far more than just ticking off tasks on a to-do list. Productivity is an art and science, blending efficient work habits with mindful living. Throughout this discussion, you have unfolded various layers of productivity, from planning and goal setting to embracing early mornings and mindful work reattachment.

The Heart of Productivity: Purpose and Planning

At the core of productivity lie the twin pillars of purposeful planning and goal alignment. You've learned that starting each day with a clear plan and a mindful reattachment to work sets a positive tone for productive endeavors. Aligning daily tasks with long-term goals ensures that your efforts contribute meaningfully to your overarching aspirations.

Maximizing Efficiency with Time Management

Effective time management, such as waking up early and adhering to deadlines, proves to be instrumental in boosting productivity. These practices help carve out quiet periods of high focus and establish a rhythm of work that maximizes efficiency.

Balancing Work with Self-Care

One of the most critical insights is the importance of balancing diligent work with self-care. Prioritizing activities like meditation, exercise, or hobbies is not a luxury but a necessity. It prevents burnout and replenishes our mental and physical reserves, enabling sustained productivity.

Overcoming Perfectionism and Embracing Growth

You also tackled the pitfalls of perfectionism and the importance of cultivating a growth mindset. Recognizing that "good enough" often trumps "perfect" allows you to move forward with tasks without getting mired in unattainable standards. A growth mindset fosters resilience, encouraging you to view challenges and setbacks as opportunities for learning and development.

Harnessing Technology and Regular Goal Reviews

Leveraging technology wisely and conducting regular reviews of your goals emerged as key strategies. They ensure that you stay on course and adapt your methods and objectives in response to changing circumstances.

In essence, productivity is a holistic approach to work and life. It's about working smarter—not harder—and ensuring that your efforts lead to meaningful achievements and personal fulfillment. As you integrate these principles into your life, you move toward a more productive, balanced, and satisfying existence. The journey of enhancing productivity is continuous, and by applying these insights, you set yourself up for a life characterized by effective work, personal growth, and well-being.

Chapter Six

Navigating Obstacles with a Grin

In this chapter, you'll dive into the inevitable: life's challenges. From the day you take your first breath to every monumental step thereafter, life throws you into a labyrinth of hurdles. These challenges, regardless of their magnitude, are the crucibles in which your resilience and strength are forged.

The Many Faces of Challenges

Life's obstacles are as diverse as they are relentless. They manifest in various forms—physical, emotional, mental, and social. Physical challenges might entail health issues or disabilities that test your endurance and adaptability. Emotional challenges could range from battling the shadows of grief and anxiety to the relentless grip of depression. Mental challenges often surface as academic or intellectual puzzles that demand our utmost focus and ingenuity. Social challenges, on the other hand, involve the complex dynamics of fitting into communities or navigating the treacherous waters of interpersonal relationships.

Financial Hurdles and Relationship Mazes

One universal challenge that resonates with many is the daunting realm of finances. Struggling to pay bills, wrestling with debt, or stretching a thin budget can be a source of constant stress and worry, casting a shadow over your well-being.

Then, there's the intricate dance of relationships. Romantic entanglements, friendships, family dynamics—each one a unique puzzle, demanding a careful balance of empathy, understanding, and patience. You are a tapestry of personalities, communication styles, and emotional needs, making the art of relationship-building both challenging and rewarding.

Academic and Professional Obstacles

In the realms of academia and career, challenges take on a more tangible form. The pressure of exams, the nerve-racking process of job interviews, or the daily grind under a demanding boss are trials that test your mental agility and resilience. Here, the image of impostor syndrome often looms large, whispering doubts and fears into your ears.

Confronting the Dragon of Fear

Arguably, the most formidable adversary you face in your quest for growth and success is fear. It's a shapeshifting dragon, capable of paralyzing even the bravest souls. Fear of failure, rejection, or the unknown can chain you to your comfort zones, inhibiting your ability to dream big and take risks.

You Are Not Alone

As you navigate this labyrinth of life's challenges, it's crucial to remember—you are not alone in this struggle. Every person faces their own battles, and it's perfectly okay to seek support. In this chapter, you'll explore strategies to tackle these diverse challenges head-on. You'll learn how to turn these obstacles into stepping-stones, transforming fear into fuel for your journey. By the end of this chapter, you'll be equipped with the tools to not just face your challenges but to embrace them as opportunities for growth and self-discovery. Let's evolve by turning life's challenges into triumphs!

The Healing Power of Laughter

Now let's delve into a seemingly simple yet profoundly transformative tool: laughter. This chapter focuses on the art of laughter, a potent force that transcends mere amusement and becomes a bridge to connection, resilience, and joy.

Laughter: A Universal Currency

Laughter, as eloquently stated by author and TED speaker Mo Barrett, is a universal currency, rich in its ability to unify and uplift. It's a language that knows no boundaries, a shared melody that resonates in every heart. Mo's words remind you that laughter isn't just about the act itself—it's about the shared experience and the communal joy it brings.

Scientific Insights into Laughter

Research underscores the profound impact of laughter on our well-being. It's not just a burst of giggles—it's a wellness tool. Studies, like the one conducted by the Hospital de Clinicas in Porto Alegre in Brazil and presented at the 2023 annual meeting of the European Society of Cardiology in Amsterdam, have highlighted laughter's role in reducing stress, boosting the immune system, and even improving cardiovascular health. Laughter releases endorphins, our body's natural feel-good chemicals, turning moments of joy into a healing balm for both mind and body.

Laughter as a Social Glue

Beyond its health benefits, laughter serves as a powerful social adhesive. It dissolves barriers, fosters camaraderie, and cultivates an atmosphere of openness and authenticity. As Mo insightfully observed, laughter connects you deeply with those who share in our mirth, forging bonds that are both genuine and enduring.

Laughter is the Best Medicine

During life's trials, a dash of humor can shed new light on daunting situations. It's like a beacon in the darkness, guiding you through rough waters with a lighter heart. Laughter enables you to find silver linings in the storm clouds of life, allowing you to approach challenges not with a heavy heart but with a hopeful spirit.

Incorporating Laughter into Your Life

The invitation here is clear: weave laughter into the fabric of your daily life. Seek out those moments of joy, whether through a hilarious video, a shared joke, or just the quirky humor of everyday life. Surround yourself with people who sparkle with laughter and strive to be a source of joy for others.

As you navigate the professional and personal aspects of your life, do not underestimate the power of laughter. It's not just a fleeting chuckle—it's a tool for building resilience, forging connections, and promoting personal growth. Let laughter be your ally in making sh** happen, lifting your spirits, and those around you, as you journey toward success.

Tackling Challenges with Grace

Life, in its unpredictable nature, often tosses curveballs your way. One moment, you're on a high, feeling like you've mastered the game; the next, you're thrown off balance by an unexpected challenge. But fear not, for these obstacles are not unattainable. This chapter is dedicated to equipping you with strategies to stay centered and calm, even in the eye of the storm.

Make a Plan

The first step in overcoming any challenge is planning. Reflect on past experiences to identify patterns and recurring hurdles. By understanding these, you can develop strategies to navigate future challenges more effectively. If you're a student, this could mean honing time management skills. For professionals, it might involve anticipating workplace challenges and crafting strategies to address them.

Know You're Not Alone

Remember, you're part of a vast community. Everyone faces their share of lows. Connecting with others, sharing experiences, and learning from their journeys can provide comfort and insight. You're part of a tapestry of shared human experiences, and in that, there's immense strength.

Ask For Help

Asking for help is a sign of strength, not weakness. Whether it's advice from a mentor, support from a friend, or guidance from a loved one, there are people ready and willing to help you navigate your challenges. Don't hesitate to reach out.

Feel Your Feelings

Emotions are not obstacles; they are guides. Allow yourself to feel, whether it's through meditation, journaling, or simply being with your emotions. Recognizing and accepting your feelings can offer new perspectives and solutions.

Accept Support

Once you've reached out for help, be open to receiving it. The people who offer their support genuinely care for your well-being. Embrace their assistance with gratitude.

Help Others

In helping others, you can find strength for yourself. Share your experiences and offer support, and you'll find that in the process, you're also bolstering your resilience and happiness.

Think Big

Don't let fear of failure cage your aspirations. Dream big, take calculated risks, and open yourself to the vast potential of what you can achieve. It's in thinking big that you often find the most innovative solutions to your challenges.

Don't Give Up

Persistence is key to overcoming challenges. Whether it's a daunting exam or a personal goal, don't back down. Use your support system, understand your emotions, and keep pushing forward.

Work Smart, Not Hard

Efficiency is often more effective than sheer effort. Define your goals, research successful strategies, and tailor them to your unique situation. Sometimes, the smart approach can save time and yield better results.

Define and Set Goals for Success

The first step is defining what success means to you. This might seem straightforward, but it's a task that requires introspection and honesty. Ask yourself: What does success look like for you? What are your personal and professional aspirations? Once you have clarity on your desired outcomes, you can begin crafting goals that are both realistic and achievable.

Break Down Goals

Consider breaking down larger goals into smaller, more manageable objectives. If you aspire to a promotion, focus first on enhancing specific skills or contributing more significantly to team projects. If personal health is a goal, set achievable milestones in exercise and nutrition. The key is to ensure that these goals are specific and actionable.

Plan for Success

With your goals set, the next step is to develop a plan of action. This involves identifying the steps necessary to achieve your goals, the resources required, and potential obstacles you might encounter. A well-thought-out plan not only increases your chances of success but also helps you stay focused and motivated.

Embrace the Journey

Remember, success is a journey filled with continuous learning and adaptation. You will encounter setbacks, but these should not deter you. Keep your eyes on the prize and maintain your resolve. Hard work, coupled with determination, is the formula for making your goals a reality.

Understand and Accept Challenges

Challenges are an integral part of life and present opportunities for growth. When faced with obstacles, it's important to maintain a positive mindset and see these challenges as stepping-stones rather than roadblocks. Recognize that you are not alone in this journey, and there are countless resources and support systems available to assist you.

Overcome Personal Obstacles

Everyone faces personal hurdles, but the difference between succumbing and overcoming lies in your approach. Cultivating a positive mindset, being action-oriented, leaning on your support system, and persevering through tough times are key traits of those who successfully navigate personal challenges.

Develop a Positive Mindset

A positive mindset is essential for success. This doesn't happen overnight but requires conscious effort. Practice gratitude, engage in positive self-talk, focus on finding solutions, surround yourself with positivity, and take care of your physical and emotional well-being. These steps will train your mind to see the brighter side and approach life with optimism and confidence.

Understand Failures as Stepping-Stones

Failure is not the opposite of success—it's a part of it. Each failure is a lesson in disguise, offering valuable insights that can pave the way to success. When you encounter failure, it's essential to take a step back and analyze what happened. Reflect on the choices you made and consider what could have been done differently. Identifying the lessons from your failures is a key step in ensuring you don't repeat the same mistakes.

Accept and Grow from Failure

Accepting failure can be challenging, but it's a necessary step toward personal growth. Embrace your failures not as defeats but as opportunities to become a stronger and wiser version of yourself. Use these experiences as tools for self-improvement and growth.

Build Resilience

Resilience is your ability to bounce back from setbacks and failures. It's a skill that can be developed over time and involves several key practices:

- Prioritize Sleep: Adequate rest is essential for mental and physical well-being, helping you better cope with stress and challenges.

- Maintain a Healthy Diet: Nutritious eating fuels your body and mind, giving you the strength to face life's hurdles.

- Regular Exercise: Physical activity releases endorphins, boosting your mood and reducing stress.

- Take Breaks: Recognize when you're overwhelmed, and allow yourself time to rest and recharge.

- Seek Social Support: Lean on your social network for emotional support, and consider professional help if needed.

- Practice Self-Care: Engage in activities that bring you joy, and don't hesitate to ask for help when necessary.

- Stay Positive: Cultivate a positive outlook, practice gratitude, and find reasons to laugh and enjoy life, even in tough times.

Setting and achieving goals is not just about the end result but about the journey. It involves understanding your definition of success, breaking down goals, planning strategically, and maintaining a positive outlook through the challenges. By adopting these strategies, you set yourself on a path toward not just achieving your goals but also experiencing personal growth and fulfillment.

Managing Stress and Anxiety

Managing stress and anxiety is an integral part of navigating the road to success. Prolonged stress can have adverse health effects, so it's important to develop strategies to manage it:

- Mindfulness Practices: Yoga and meditation can be effective in finding inner peace and reducing stress.

- Engage in Enjoyable Activities: Allocate time for hobbies and activities that bring you joy and relaxation.

- Open Communication: Talk about your stress and anxiety with friends, family, or a therapist for support and understanding.

Celebrating Accomplishments

Celebrating your achievements is crucial in maintaining motivation and enthusiasm on your journey:

- Take a Break: Reward yourself with some time off to relax and rejuvenate.

- Share Your Success: Communicate your accomplishments through blogs, presentations, or conversations with friends and family.

- Reward Yourself: Treat yourself to something special as a recognition of your hard work and achievements.

Up to now, you have explored the importance of learning from failures, building resilience, managing stress, and celebrating accomplishments. Remember, the path to success is not linear—it's a journey filled with ups and downs. By embracing failures as learning opportunities, building resilience, effectively managing stress, and taking time to celebrate your achievements, you equip yourself with the tools necessary for a successful and fulfilling journey. Continue to make sh** happen by turning every setback into a step forward toward your goals.

Understanding Perseverance

Perseverance transcends mere motivation and determination, encompassing elements of both. It involves persisting through discomfort and overcoming obstacles. This concept is closely linked to your capacity for delaying gratification, exercising self-regulation, and practicing self-control. In essence, perseverance is about prioritizing sustainable, long-term rewards over immediate gratification.

The Role of Perseverance in Learning and Mastery

Every learning process and journey toward mastery is underpinned by perseverance. From learning to speak or walk to mastering a musical instrument or a new language, perseverance is the engine driving your progress. Without it, your cognitive, physical, and psychosocial development would stagnate, leaving you unable to move forward or overcome your limitations.

Personality Traits and Perseverance

Perseverance is a dynamic blend of continuous effort, purposefulness, and goal-setting driven by passion and a commitment to long-term goals. However, perseverance is not just a behavior but can also be seen as a personality or temperamental trait, linked to effort, ambition, and even perfectionism. In the realm of personality psychology, particularly the Big Five or Five-Factor Model, perseverance aligns closely with conscientiousness, which encompasses goal setting, self-discipline, orderliness, and carefulness.

Perseverance as a Character Strength: Grit

The concept of grit, as popularized by psychologist Angela Duckworth, encapsulates the combination of perseverance and passion. Grit is not just an innate quality but a dispositional tendency that can be developed and nurtured. Duckworth's research underscores that while natural talent is valuable, perseverance and continual effort often play a more significant role in achieving success.

Grit in Academic and Professional Contexts

In academic settings, individuals with higher levels of grit often outperform their peers, achieving better grades and higher levels of educational attainment. This correlation between grit and success extends beyond academics into various professional and personal contexts.

Developing Grit and Perseverance

The encouraging news is that grit and perseverance are not static traits; instead, they can be cultivated and strengthened over time. By consciously practicing perseverance, setting long-term goals, and maintaining passion and focus, you can enhance your ability to succeed in various aspects of your life.

In summary, perseverance, or grit, is a pivotal component in the pursuit of success. It requires a combination of continuous effort, discipline, and passion.

The Psychology of Resilience

Resilience, the ability to cope with adversity and bounce back from challenges, is not an inherent trait but a dynamic process. It's about growing from stress, trauma, and change, not just surviving them. Resilience involves finding meaning in adversity and using it as a catalyst for growth and development.

Characteristics of Resilient Individuals

Recognizing its psychological underpinnings is key to cultivating resilience. Resilient individuals typically exhibit several defining characteristics:

Optimistic Outlook

Resilient people tend to focus on positive outcomes and believe in their capacity to influence events. Cultivate optimism by acknowledging daily achievements, however small, and maintaining a balanced perspective on life's challenges.

Growth Mindset

Individuals with a growth mindset view their abilities as malleable and improvable through effort. They perceive failure as a learning opportunity. You can develop this mindset by embracing challenges, learning from setbacks, and nurturing a love for lifelong learning and self-improvement.

Strong Self-Efficacy

Those with high self-efficacy have a firm belief in their ability to succeed. They see obstacles as possible with enough motivation and perseverance. Enhance your self-efficacy by setting and achieving small goals and reflecting on past successes and strengths.

Adaptability

Resilience is closely tied to adaptability—the ability to adjust to new conditions. Resilient individuals can assess situations objectively and find creative solutions to problems. Boost your adaptability by exposing yourself to new ideas, learning new skills, or engaging in unfamiliar activities.

Connection to Purpose

Having a sense of purpose and meaning is a cornerstone of resilience. Resilient individuals often have goals and motivations that extend beyond themselves. Identify your purpose and seek out communities or individuals with similar values to strengthen your resilience.

Building a Resilient Mindset

Developing resilience is a journey of personal growth that requires dedication and practice. It involves fostering an optimistic and growth-oriented outlook, building a strong sense of self-efficacy, honing your adaptability skills, and connecting with a deeper sense of purpose. This journey also involves staying motivated and persistent in the face of challenges, enabling you to overcome obstacles and reach greater heights in life.

Conclusion

You started by delving into the transformative power of mindset. Understanding the difference between a fixed and growth mindset sets the stage for how you approach challenges and opportunities in life. By adopting a growth mindset, you open yourself to endless possibilities of learning and advancement.

Overcoming Challenges and Learning from Failures

Life's labyrinth of challenges, as you discovered, is not a roadblock but a series of stepping-stones toward personal growth. Embracing these challenges, learning from failures, and developing resilience are crucial steps in your journey. Each obstacle faced and overcome strengthens your resolve and hones your skills.

The Role of Perseverance and Resilience

Perseverance and resilience emerged as key themes throughout your journey. These are not just innate qualities but skills that can be cultivated. By embracing perseverance, you learn the value of continuous effort and determination. Through understanding the psychology of resilience, you equip yourself to bounce back from adversity and grow stronger from your experiences.

In conclusion, *Making Sh** Happen* is more than just a guide; it's a mindset, a way of life. It's about recognizing that the journey to achieving big results is filled with learning, growth, and the ability to bounce back from setbacks. It's about understanding that minimal effort does not mean a lack of effort but rather the efficient and effective channeling of your energies toward your goals.

This journey requires a blend of self-awareness, discipline, and a willingness to step out of your comfort zone. By harnessing the power of your mind, embracing your failures as lessons, building resilience, and persevering against all odds, you set yourself up for success in all facets of life.

Remember, the path to efficiency is not linear; it's a winding road filled with ups and downs. But with the right tools, mindset, and determination, you can navigate this path and emerge victorious. Here's to making sh** happen in your life and achieving your dreams with insight, wisdom, and a dash of audacity.

Chapter Seven

The Art of Networking and Building Relationships

If you want to really get things done, mastering the art of networking is a crucial skill. In the business world and beyond, the ability to build and maintain relationships is invaluable. Networking isn't just about expanding your contact list; it's about forging meaningful connections that can lead to opportunities, growth, and mutual benefits. Let's dive deeper into the essence of networking and explore strategies to make your networking efforts fruitful and lasting.

Understanding Networking

Effective networking is about more than exchanging business cards or adding contacts on social media. It's a strategic effort to cultivate relationships that go beyond initial meetings. This involves creating genuine, mutually beneficial connections that are nurtured over time.

Networking is an investment in building rapport that can be a significant asset in both personal and career development. Strong, enduring connections can unlock doors to new opportunities, offer valuable insights, and foster a sense of community among like-minded individuals and groups.

The Purpose of Networking

To network effectively, understanding its purpose is key. Networking is not just about self-promotion or seeking immediate benefits. It's about establishing a symbiotic relationship where both parties can contribute value. Whether you're in search of guidance, collaboration, mentorship, or career opportunities, having a clear objective in mind can steer your networking efforts in the right direction.

Keys to Effective Networking

Authenticity: Genuine interactions are the foundation of effective networking. Be yourself and let your true personality and intentions shine through in your interactions.

Active Listening and Engagement: Pay close attention to what others say. Showing genuine interest in their ideas, needs, and concerns can help build a deeper connection.

Helping Others: Networking is reciprocal. Offer your knowledge, resources, or assistance to others. This not only strengthens your connections but also establishes you as a valuable and reliable contact.

Consistent Communication: Take the initiative to reach out, follow up, and maintain contact. Consistent communication is essential in nurturing your network.

Long-Term Perspective: Focus on building relationships that have the potential to grow over time. Networking is a long-term endeavor, not a one-time transaction.

Diversify Your Network: Expand your network across different industries, professions, and backgrounds. This diversity can bring new perspectives and opportunities.

Leverage Technology: Utilize social media platforms, professional networking sites, and digital tools to connect with others, especially in today's digital age.

Attend Events and Conferences: Participating in industry events, conferences, and workshops is a great way to meet new people and strengthen existing connections.

Be a Connector: Introduce people in your network to each other. Being a connector not only helps others but also enhances your value within your network.

Follow Up and Follow Through: After meeting someone new, follow up with a message or email. If you promised to share information or make an introduction, do so promptly.

Networking is an art that requires patience, strategy, and genuine interest in others. By approaching networking with the right mindset and skills, you can build a robust network that supports your personal and professional growth. Remember, effective networking is about creating meaningful relationships, not just expanding your list of contacts. It's about contributing to others' success as much as it is about enhancing your own. Embrace these principles, and watch as your network becomes a powerful catalyst for productivity.

Importance of Healthy Social Relationships in Achieving Goals

In your efforts to achieve your goals, you often emphasize individual traits like hard work, concentration, and willpower. However, one crucial aspect that tends to be overlooked in goal setting is the power of healthy social relationships.

The Underestimated Power of Support Systems

The significance of a strong support system in achieving goals cannot be overstated. Research highlights that individuals who share their goals and progress with others are considerably more successful in their endeavors. Healthy social relationships are not just about leisure activities; they play a pivotal role in mutual learning and growth. The encouragement from friends and loved ones is invaluable, especially when facing challenges.

While the ultimate responsibility of achieving your goals rests with you, having a supportive network can provide the necessary emotional and motivational sustenance throughout your journey.

Engaging Others in Your Goal Journey

Once you have identified your goals, share them with someone you trust—a friend, family member, or a community member. This does two things: first, it makes your goals feel more real and achievable, and second, it creates a sense of accountability. Arrange for regular check-ins with this person, which could include updates on your progress and discussions on any challenges faced.

The Role of Specificity in Accountability

When involving others in your goal-setting process, be specific about the nature of their involvement. Determine how and how often they will check in with you. This clarity will help maintain a focused and effective support system.

Building a Network for Success

Expand your network to include people who share similar goals or have expertise in areas you're pursuing. This can provide additional motivation, insights, and opportunities for collaboration.

In summary, while individual traits like determination and self-discipline are vital for achieving goals, the role of healthy social relationships is equally important. These relationships provide emotional support, accountability, and valuable perspectives. Remember, the journey needn't be a solitary endeavor—it's a path that can be enriched and supported by the relationships you nurture along the way.

Tips for Building Lasting Connections

It's time to explore the often-overlooked, lighter side of networking. Networking doesn't need to be a tedious task—it can be as enjoyable as your favorite hobby, with the right approach and a sprinkle of humor. Here are twenty-three tips to help you build stronger, more meaningful connections.

Craft a Stand-Out Resumé

Your resumé is like your personal billboard. It should highlight your skills and achievements in a way that captures attention. Use modern tools to create a resumé that pops. Share it at networking events and online, where it can catch the eye of potential connections and opportunities.

Embrace Authenticity

In the world of networking, being genuine is your ace card. People connect with those who are real and relatable. Authentic connections last longer and are more fulfilling. So, drop the façade and let your true personality shine.

Diversify Your Network

Don't just stick to familiar faces and places. Branch out and connect with people from different industries, cultures, and backgrounds. A diverse network brings fresh perspectives and unexpected opportunities, much like a great mystery novel full of surprising twists and turns.

Be a Great Listener

Listening is a networking superpower. Show genuine interest in what others have to say. Ask engaging questions and listen actively. People appreciate being heard and will remember you for making them feel valued.

Offer Value

Networking is not just about what you can get but also about what you can give. Share your knowledge, offer help, and connect people in your network. This generosity not only strengthens your connections but also sets you apart as a valuable contact.

Attend Select Networking Events

Be strategic about the networking events you attend. Choose those that align with your goals and interests. At these events, be engaging, curious, and approachable, much like a great host at a dinner party.

Utilize Social Media

Platforms like LinkedIn, X (Twitter), and Instagram are powerful networking tools. Create a compelling online presence that showcases your expertise and interests. Engage with others by sharing content, commenting on posts, and making meaningful connections.

Master Follow-up Skills

Building a connection is just the beginning. To grow these relationships, you need to follow up effectively. Send personalized messages, make calls, and check in with your network regularly. Be the one who remembers to reach out.

Practice Patience

Building meaningful connections takes time. Don't be discouraged by initial setbacks. Stay persistent and continue nurturing your relationships. Over time, your network will grow and become more valuable.

Seek a Mentor

Finding a mentor can accelerate your personal and professional growth. Look for individuals who inspire you and ask them for guidance. Be clear about what you want from the relationship, and be proactive in learning and growing from their advice.

Prioritize Quality over Quantity

When building valuable relationships, always ask, "What can I bring to the table?" Effective networking is a two-way street where value is exchanged. Sending generic requests for help won't cut it. Instead, send a message that offers a solution to a problem your contact might have and how your skills can contribute to the solution.

Make the Most of Your First Impression

First impressions are like opening scenes in a blockbuster movie—they set the tone. To make a lasting positive impression, polish your communication skills and get to the point. Show genuine interest in the other person because, let's face it, everyone loves talking about themselves.

Follow Up without Stalking

Patience is key in the world of networking. Sometimes, messages go unanswered due to busy schedules or forgetfulness. After 3–5 days of no response, consider a friendly follow-up. Just remember, there's a fine line between persistence and stalking, so tread lightly.

Listen Actively

Listening is your secret weapon in building authentic connections. People remember how you made them feel, and being genuinely interested in their perspective goes a long way. Show interest in your contact's life, and you'll instantly win them over.

Don't Multitask

When building quality relationships, it's better to focus your energy on a select few rather than spreading yourself thin. Identify the relationships that matter most, prioritize them, and avoid multitasking, which can drain your energy.

Hone Your Conversational Skills

Great conversations are the glue that holds relationships together. To sharpen your conversational skills, take your time, maintain eye contact, notice the little details about the other person, offer insightful insights, and, above all, listen more than you talk.

Occasionally Act as a Conduit

Networking isn't just about what you can gain; it's also about what you can give. Introduce people to each other from time to time. Expanding your network and creating goodwill can lead to unexpected opportunities.

Maintain Open-Mindedness

Not everyone will share your values or outlook. Open-mindedness is your superpower in navigating differences. Embrace diverse perspectives as opportunities to learn and grow.

Remind, Reinforce, and Check In

Consistency is key to maintaining relationships. Stay on your contacts' radar by sending short notes, congratulating them on their achievements, and simply inquiring about their well-being.

Uphold Your Reputation

A clean reputation is a valuable asset in networking. Avoid unnecessary controversies and troublemaking behavior, as nobody wants to associate with a source of drama.

Diversify Your Networking

Cast a wide net in your networking efforts. Connect not only with those in your industry but also with peers and individuals from diverse backgrounds.

Show Gratitude

Express your appreciation regularly. Send thank-you notes, publicly acknowledge their contributions, and even surprise them with flowers. These small gestures go a long way in showing you value the relationship.

Monitor Your Networking Progress

Document your relationship-building activities to stay organized and keep track of your contacts. This template will help you maintain a detailed record of your networking efforts.

By implementing these strategies, you'll master the art of building strong relationships that benefit not only you but those around you as well. Keep nurturing connections, and your dream career might just become a reality sooner than you think.

Mastering the art of networking is about more than just exchanging contact information. It's about creating and nurturing relationships that are both beneficial and enjoyable. Step out of your comfort zone, embrace new opportunities, and remember the best connections are the ones where both sides benefit. Here's to networking your way to success with a smile!

The Benefits of Networking

While it may seem like just another professional activity, networking has the potential to transform your career and personal growth in ways you might not have imagined. So, grab your networking toolkit and get ready to explore the incredible advantages that come with building and nurturing relationships in the professional world.

The Networking Ecosystem

Think of networking as your own thriving ecosystem, one where you connect, share, and collaborate with a diverse range of individuals. This ecosystem includes not only your colleagues and business connections but also friends, family, and even the members of the various groups you belong to. It's a dynamic network that can have a profound impact on your life.

Strengthening Business Connections: Networking isn't just about taking; it's about sharing and building trust. When you engage with your contacts and actively seek opportunities to assist them, you lay the foundation for reciprocal assistance. Your network becomes a web of support, ready to help you when you need it most.

Getting Fresh Ideas: Your network is a wellspring of new perspectives and innovative ideas. Through conversations with your connections, you gain insights and viewpoints you might not have encountered otherwise. Sharing your own ideas also positions you as an innovative thinker, contributing to the collective pool of knowledge.

Advancing Your Career: In the professional world, visibility is key. By actively participating in networking events and social gatherings, you become a familiar face. Establishing yourself as a knowledgeable, reliable, and supportive individual can open doors to new career opportunities and advancement.

Access to New Information: Networking provides a unique opportunity to exchange knowledge and stay updated on industry trends. Your diverse network ensures that you have access to a wealth of information and insights, keeping you ahead of the curve.

Career Advice and Support: Seeking advice from experienced peers is a valuable aspect of networking. Discussing common challenges and opportunities allows you to tap into the wisdom of your network, receiving valuable suggestions and guidance. Offering help to your contacts also lays the groundwork for receiving support when you need it.

Building Confidence: Networking pushes you out of your comfort zone and helps you develop essential social skills and self-confidence. The more you engage with new people, the more you grow, gaining the ability to establish lasting connections.

Gaining a Different Perspective: It's easy to become stuck in your professional routine. Networking with others in your field or experts in specific areas can provide fresh insights. Seeking opinions from trusted contacts can help you overcome obstacles and view challenges from a new angle.

Developing Personal Relationships: While the primary goal of networking is professional, some of the strongest and most enduring friendships can arise from these connections. Shared goals and interests often lead to personal friendships, enriching both your personal and professional life.

Access to Answers: With a robust professional network, you're never far from finding answers to your questions. Your contacts provide a valuable resource for knowledge and problem-solving, ensuring that even the toughest questions can be addressed.

Discovering Your Dream Job: Networking expands your horizons and creates opportunities. Your extensive network increases the likelihood of being the first to hear about ideal job openings. Whether it's career advancement, personal growth, or new knowledge, professional networking can be the key to unlocking these opportunities.

So, as you embark on this journey through the world of networking, keep in mind the incredible benefits that await. Networking isn't just about making connections; it's about nurturing relationships that can shape your professional and personal life in ways you never thought possible.

Conclusion

In conclusion, the benefits of networking in achieving success are undeniable and far-reaching. Networking is not merely a professional activity; it is a strategic pathway to personal and career growth. Through the power of networking, individuals can unlock a multitude of advantages that contribute to their success.

First and foremost, networking strengthens business connections by fostering trust and reciprocity. It creates a support system where individuals can rely on one another to achieve their goals. This interconnected web of relationships becomes a valuable asset in navigating the complexities of the professional world.

Networking also serves as a wellspring of fresh ideas and perspectives. Engaging with diverse individuals exposes you to innovative thinking and novel solutions to challenges. By actively participating in this exchange of ideas, you position yourself as an innovative thinker, further enhancing your professional reputation.

Furthermore, networking is a crucial component of career advancement. Visibility is key in the professional realm, and networking events provide opportunities to become known as a knowledgeable and supportive individual. This increased visibility can open doors to new career prospects and personal growth.

Access to information is another significant benefit of networking. In a rapidly changing world, staying informed about industry trends and best practices is essential. A robust network ensures that you have access to a wealth of knowledge and insights, giving you a competitive edge.

Seeking advice and support from experienced peers is an invaluable aspect of networking. Engaging in conversations about common challenges and opportunities can lead to valuable guidance and suggestions. Offering assistance to your contacts establishes a foundation for receiving support when you need it most.

Networking also contributes to personal development by building confidence and social skills. Stepping out of your comfort zone and meeting new people is a transformative experience. The more you network, the more you grow, equipping yourself with the ability to establish lasting connections.

Moreover, networking offers a fresh perspective on your professional journey. It prevents stagnation and encourages continuous growth by exposing you to different viewpoints and approaches. Seeking advice from trusted contacts can help you overcome obstacles and find new solutions.

Last, networking can lead to the development of personal relationships that enrich both your personal and professional life. Shared goals and interests often result in deep, long-lasting friendships that provide emotional support and fulfillment.

In the world of networking, answers are always within reach. Your extensive network ensures that even the most challenging questions can be addressed, and together, you can tackle complex problems and seize new opportunities.

Ultimately, networking is the key to discovering your dream job, advancing your career, and achieving personal and professional success. By actively participating in this dynamic ecosystem of connections, you can harness its remarkable benefits to propel yourself toward your goals. So, embrace the power of networking, nurture your relationships, and watch as they pave the way to your success.

Chapter Eight

Cultivating Grit and Determination

Welcome to the exploration of two remarkable qualities that serve as the bedrock of achievement: grit and determination. Grit is the inner fire that fuels your passion for long-term objectives, while determination is the unyielding resolve that propels you toward your goals. In the journey to success, these two traits act as your unwavering companions, guiding you through challenges, setbacks, and triumphs.

The Power of Grit and Determination

Picture this scenario: a person's life takes a nosedive, and they find themselves at rock bottom. Yet, from the depths of despair, they summon their inner strength and unleash an unyielding determination to rebuild what was lost. This resolute spirit becomes their driving force, propelling them toward their goals.

The truth is that you possess this same power within you. Regardless of life's challenges and curveballs, you have the capacity to tap into your reservoir of inner strength and willpower. Armed with grit and determination, you can conquer any obstacle that dares to stand in your way.

Understanding Grit and Determination

To embark on the path to success, you must acquaint yourself with grit and determination. Grit is your relentless passion, akin to a burning fire that sustains you through adversity. It's the unwavering motivation that drives you forward, even when the odds seem impossible.

Think of grit as the force that keeps you going when your friends abandon your cause or when your family questions your choices. It's the tenacity to persist when quitting appears to be the easiest option. Grit is about refusing to surrender, even when the path ahead is shrouded in darkness.

Determination, on the other hand, is the unwavering willpower that propels you toward your objectives. It's the unshakable belief that you can and will achieve what you set out to do. Determination declares, "I am going to do this," with unwavering resolve.

Together, grit and determination form an unstoppable alliance, capable of overcoming any obstacle and achieving the loftiest of goals.

The Relationship between Grit and Determination

Grit and determination are not solitary entities—they are intricately intertwined. The Merriam-Webster dictionary defines grit as "firmness of mind or spirit: unyielding courage in the face of hardship or danger" and determination as "firm or fixed intention to achieve a desired end." These definitions reveal the symbiotic nature of these two qualities, both of which are indispensable for success.

Grit represents the amalgamation of determination and passion. It's the capacity to persevere through arduous tasks and unyielding goals, even when the journey becomes arduous. Grit enables individuals to press on in the face of adversity, and it is this unrelenting perseverance that leads to success.

Determination, on the other hand, embodies the commitment to persist in the face of failure. Individuals with determination possess an unwavering sense of purpose and an unswerving focus on surmounting obstacles. They understand that their desires are nonnegotiable, and no challenge can deter them.

The connection between grit and determination is undeniable. Determination acts as the catalyst for grit, laying the foundation for unwavering perseverance. Those with determination exhibit higher levels of grit, allowing them to navigate the tumultuous waters of life with unwavering resolve.

The Crucial Role of Grit and Determination in Achieving Success

Grit and determination are the backbone of success. In your pursuit of goals, there are moments when you feel vulnerable and uncertain. It's during these times that your inner reservoirs of determination can empower you to push your boundaries. These qualities not only give you the strength to take risks but also equip you to confront your fears head-on. Therefore, it is paramount that you not only possess but also nurture these attributes within yourself.

Drawing inspiration from individuals who faced daunting challenges and persevered until they reached their dreams can be immensely motivating. Their stories serve as a testament to the boundless strength and unwavering determination that humans can harness. They remind you that, regardless of the obstacles in your path, you have the potential to cultivate the courage needed to pursue your aspirations.

By tapping into your reserves of grit and determination, you can foster an attitude that screams, "I can overcome anything." This attitude becomes the driving force that propels you forward and helps you make steady progress toward your goals.

The Significance of Grit in the Path to Success

Grit is the glue that keeps you committed to your goals. When you embark on a journey toward your objectives, you understand that it won't always be smooth sailing. However, with an ample supply of grit, you can weather the storms and continue your voyage without faltering. It enables you to persist in the face of adversity, ensuring that you don't abandon your goals halfway. Achieving excellence often demands unwavering dedication, which means setting aside time each day to diligently work toward your objectives.

Author Angela Duckworth, in her book *Grit*, aptly likens grit to a muscle that needs consistent development and strengthening. She underscores the significance of recognizing your weaknesses and emphasizes the incremental changes necessary to fortify your capacity for grit and determination.

Grit is not just a quality—it's a mindset. It necessitates the formulation of a strategic plan and a realistic outlook. Self-awareness and self-compassion play pivotal roles in your ability to tap into your inner strength effortlessly.

Those who possess grit persevere where others might surrender. It is the driving force that compels you to press on even when faced with daunting challenges. Grit ensures that you stick to your plan and remain resolute in your decision-making, even when faced with tough choices or distractions.

In essence, grit is the amalgamation of passion, patience, and perseverance. It embodies the ability to persist tirelessly, even when the journey becomes arduous. While the temptation to quit may arise when things aren't going smoothly, grit enables you to push forward steadfastly.

To nurture grit, one must invest time and effort in personal growth consistently. The reward for such dedication is the ability to stand unwavering in the face of adversity.

The Vital Role of Determination in Achieving Success

Determination is the key that unlocks the door to success, but knowing how to harness it is crucial. Determination is synonymous with the willingness to exert relentless effort in pursuit of one's aspirations.

Success is impossible without determination. It empowers individuals to surmount obstacles and make strides toward their goals. It's the unwavering resolve to celebrate the small victories in life without allowing them to hinder the pursuit of larger dreams. Looking back on life, a determined individual takes pride in having persevered through challenges, regardless of their nature.

A lack of determination can be paralyzing. Without the will to fight for one's goals, progress becomes an uphill battle. It's essential to understand that anything is achievable with determination, as long as one is willing to work diligently and invest effort in the pursuit of success.

Perseverance in the face of adversity is the hallmark of determination. Challenges may attempt to deter or impede progress, but a determined individual remains unyielding. It is crucial not to allow external influences to dictate the course of one's journey. In the face of hardships, whether favorable or unfavorable, determination ensures that every experience contributes to personal growth and resilience.

Real-Life Examples of Grit and Determination

Michael Jordan

Michael Jordan, the basketball legend, was once removed from his high school basketball team. Yes, you read that right! The guy who later became one of the greatest basketball players ever couldn't make the cut in his own high school. Talk about a slam dunk in irony! But Jordan didn't let that stop him. He famously said, "I have missed more than 9,000 shots in my career. I have failed over and over again in my life. And that is why I succeed." So, the next time you miss a shot, just remember, you're in good company.

Jack Ma

Jack Ma, born in 1964, is a Chinese entrepreneur, philanthropist, and investor. Some might be shocked to know that his journey to success reads like a comedy of errors. He really wanted to go to college, but the entrance exam seemed to have other plans for him. On his first attempt, he scored a whopping one out of 120 possible points in math. That's like trying to dunk a basketball and ending up hitting your own head! On the second try, he failed again. The third time's a charm, right? Well, he barely passed, which allowed him to enroll in a less-than-prestigious institute. Later, even Kentucky Fried Chicken rejected him when all twenty-four other applicants got in. He ended up as an English teacher, which is like taking a scenic detour on the road to success. But guess what? He stumbled upon the internet, and the rest is history. Jack Ma: from scoring one in math to becoming one of the richest people on the planet. Now, that's a plot twist.

Agatha Christie

That's right, even the queen of mystery herself was rejected at the beginning of her career. And not just once or twice but many times. Can you imagine being that publisher? Talk about hindsight. In fact, it took Agatha Christie four years to get her first book, *The Mysterious Affair at Styles*, published. Her persistence paid off, though. Now, a little over one hundred years later, Agatha Christies is the world's second best-selling fiction author. She's got an impressive collection of sixty-six mysteries, fourteen short stories, and twenty plays that have been adapted into countless radio and TV shows and movies. "Nothing turns out quite the way that you thought it would when you are sketching out notes for the first chapter, or walking about muttering to yourself and seeing a story unfold," Agatha Christie once said about her writing process. Which is so true. After being rejected by every well-known publisher of her time, the twenty-two-year-old writer likely had no idea that in four years, someone would take a chance on her. So, if you're feeling rejected, just remember, you're on the path to literary greatness. It doesn't matter how many "no's" you get; you just need that one "yes," and it might be just around the corner.

Oprah Winfrey

Oprah Winfrey's journey to stardom had a shaky start. She snagged a coveted job as a co-anchor for the evening news at Baltimore's ABC affiliate, which was a dream come true for a young journalist. But the dream quickly turned into a bumpy ride as she was dropped after just a few months. Her career took an unexpected detour to less glamorous roles like writing and street reporting. Oprah once referred to these early years as the "first and worst failure" of her TV career. Imagine being yelled at for not writing fast enough; it's like being in a race with a snail. But Oprah didn't throw in the towel. She took those tough lessons from Baltimore and used them to navigate her way to success, proving that sometimes you have to go through a few rough drafts before you write your own success story.

Walt Disney

Walt Disney, the man behind Mickey Mouse, faced his fair share of failures. He was fired from a newspaper job for having a "lack of good ideas." So, what did he do next? He decided to start his own animation company in 1921, only to watch it go bankrupt. Times got so tough that he resorted to eating dog food for survival. Yes, you read that correctly, dog food. Now, here's the punchline: Would you start another animation company after dining on dog food? Walt Disney did, and he faced more failures along the way. But he persisted, and eventually, he turned his dreams into the magical world of Disney we all know and love. So, remember, even when life serves you kibble, you can still cook up something magical.

Henry Ford

Henry Ford, the founder of Ford Motor Company, had his fair share of automotive mishaps. In 1889, he left a comfortable job to establish the Detroit Automobile Company with a hefty investment. Unfortunately, it went bankrupt in a little over a year. His investors must have been questioning their life choices at that point. But remarkably, they still had faith in Ford and supported the Henry Ford Company in 1901, which also met the same fate of bankruptcy. Now, imagine losing your investors' money not once but twice. Would you try a third time? Well, Ford did just that, founding the Ford Motor Company in 1903. Five years later, the Model T rolled off the assembly line, and the rest is automobile history. It's like saying, "I broke it twice, so let's build it thrice!"

Jay-Z

Jay-Z, the hip-hop mogul, faced rejection after rejection in the early 1990s from every record label in the business. Some thought he was too old, while others doubted his "street cred" because he didn't rap about drugs or crime. But Jay-Z didn't throw in the towel; he decided to take matters into his own hands and formed his own record label to release his first album. Fast forward, and he and his wife, Beyoncé, are worth an estimated $900 million. So, the next time someone tells you "no," just remember you're in good company with Jay-Z.

The Beatles

The legendary Beatles, who rocked the music world like no other, had a rocky start of their own. Despite enjoying local success while playing cover songs in bars and clubs across the United Kingdom, they faced rejection after rejection from record labels. In a rejection that still stings, an executive at Decca Records famously turned them down, stating, "Guitar groups are on the way out," and boldly claiming, "The Beatles have no future in show business." Ouch, indeed!

However, this rejection has since become one of the most colossal blunders in music history. Hopefully, that executive learned a valuable lesson from her epic failure. So, the next time you find yourself facing rejection, remember the Beatles' journey to stardom. It might just be that you haven't failed at all, but rather, you're on the path to greatness. And here's a twist: Two years after Decca rejected the Beatles, George Harrison returned to the label with some advice—to sign the Rolling Stones. This time, Decca learned from its past mistake and enjoyed a success of its own. It's a reminder that sometimes, failure can lead to wisdom and better decisions.

Fred Astaire

Imagine booking a screen test at MGM Studios early in your career, feeling on top of the world. Then, you receive the director's feedback, and it reads like a laundry list of shortcomings: "Can't act. Can't sing. Slightly bald. Not handsome. Can dance a little." Fred Astaire, the iconic dancer and actor, faced this harsh critique. But he didn't let it deter him. Instead, he used that note as a source of motivation and a testament to his resilience. Astaire proudly displayed it in his Beverly Hills mansion, a reminder to never take "no" for an answer. He went on to become immensely successful, proving that sometimes, all you need is a little dance in your step to overcome criticism.

Babe Ruth

Babe Ruth, often hailed as one of the greatest baseball players of all time, had a unique claim to fame. While he's renowned for his remarkable home run records, what many don't know is that he also held the record for the most strikeouts in all of Major League Baseball when he retired in 1935. Yes, you read that right—Ruth trudged back to the dugout twice as often as he ran the bases. His explanation for this apparent contradiction was nothing short of legendary: "I just go up there, and I swing. I just keep on swinging, and I keep on swinging. Every strike brings me closer to my next home run." Ruth's philosophy was a home run in itself. It reminds you that failure is just another swing on the journey to success.

These tales of triumph remind you that even in the face of setbacks, a sprinkle of humor can make the journey to success a lot more entertaining. So, keep your chin up, laugh in the face of failure, and who knows, you might just be the next legend on this list!

Developing Grit and Determination: Your Path to Success

Grit and determination are the cornerstone of achieving your goals and realizing your dreams. These qualities may not come naturally to everyone, but with dedication and practice, you can cultivate them and set yourself on a path to success. Now, let's explore how you can develop these invaluable traits.

Identify Your Weaknesses

The journey toward grit and determination begins with self-awareness. Identify your weaknesses and areas where you need improvement. Acknowledging these areas is the first step toward growth.

Set Realistic Goals

Goals serve as the compass on your path to success. Whether they're personal or professional, break them down into smaller, manageable steps. These incremental goals provide a roadmap to your ultimate destination.

Create a Concrete Plan of Action

Once you've set your goals, formulate a clear and actionable plan. Write down each step required to reach your objectives, along with deadlines. Having a well-structured plan provides direction and purpose.

Take Consistent Action

Visualize yourself making progress toward your goals by taking consistent action. Execute each step on time, even on days when motivation wanes. Discipline and consistency are key to building grit.

Embrace Setbacks and Failures

Remember that setbacks and failures are part of the journey to success. Don't let them deter you. Instead, practice self-compassion—be kind to yourself when things don't go as planned. Learn from your mistakes and keep moving forward.

Be a Lifelong Learner

Never stop learning. Reading books and acquiring new knowledge and skills are essential for personal growth. Opt for reading in your free time instead of mindlessly scrolling through social media feeds. Remember, your mind can guide you toward your goals if you give it the opportunity.

Adopt a Positive Growth Mindset

Embrace the concept of a growth mindset, believing that you can improve and grow through hard work and practice. This optimistic perspective fosters self-confidence and the belief that you can achieve your goals.

As famed Austrian psychologist Viktor Frankl wisely noted, "Between stimulus and response, there is a space. In that space is our power to choose our response. In our response lies our growth and our freedom."

So, don't shy away from challenges, setbacks, or the effort required to cultivate grit and determination. Embrace them as stepping-stones on your path to success.

Cultivate Passion for Your Work

Falling in love with your work and nurturing your passion for it can be a game-changer. Even if others don't share the same level of enthusiasm, your passion can be a powerful driving force in your life.

When you genuinely love what you do, waking up in the morning becomes a joyous endeavor. Passion infuses your work with purpose, keeping you motivated and propelling you forward, even when faced with challenges.

Passionate individuals possess a unique ability to spot opportunities everywhere, not only within their work but also in other aspects of life, including their relationships and family. They maintain a clear vision of their life's goals, helping them stay resolute when confronted with adversity.

So, make it a point to adore your work. Seek a career that resonates with your heart and soul. Then, commit to making it better with each passing day.

Embrace Honesty with Integrity

Honesty is the cornerstone of authentic connections and genuine respect from others. Being honest about your thoughts, feelings, and desires builds trust and fosters meaningful relationships. It's essential to convey your truths without resorting to rudeness or hurtfulness.

When you're honest with yourself and others, it's a powerful demonstration of your care and respect for them. Embrace honesty as a tool to strengthen bonds and create a more transparent and authentic world.

Stick to a Consistent Routine

Consistency is the foundation that keeps you focused and motivated, especially during challenging and discouraging times. As the saying goes, "The best way to predict the future is to invent it." This saying applies to your life as well.

Sticking to a routine allows you to maintain control over your life. It provides structure and predictability, making it easier to hold yourself accountable and avoid unnecessary setbacks. When you anticipate events and tasks, you can better prepare and ensure that you stay on track.

Embrace Failure as a Stepping-Stone

Building grit and resilience often involves encountering failure repeatedly, each time gleaning valuable lessons and forging ahead with renewed courage and determination. It's essential to approach failure with an open mindset, not met with anger or shame, but with a willingness to receive feedback and improve.

In essence, failure is not a dead end but a pivot point on your journey to success. It's through these moments of setback that you refine your character, strengthen your resolve, and ultimately pave the way for your triumphs.

Conclusion

In conclusion, grit and determination are not merely abstract qualities—they are the bedrock of success in any endeavor. These qualities empower individuals to persevere in the face of adversity, to set audacious goals, and to chase their dreams relentlessly. Through the stories of countless individuals who have overcome failures, setbacks, and rejection, you see that grit and determination are not reserved for a select few but are attainable by anyone willing to cultivate them.

The journey toward success is rarely a smooth path. It is often marked by trials, tribulations, and moments of doubt. However, it is those who possess grit and determination who weather these storms, learn from their failures, and emerge stronger and wiser. They understand that failure is not a destination but a stepping-stone on the path to greatness.

Ultimately, grit and determination are the driving forces that propel individuals toward their goals and dreams. They fuel the fire of ambition, inspire perseverance, and create a mindset that says, "I will not be defeated." These qualities are the true differentiators between those who achieve their aspirations and those who fall short.

So, as you navigate your own journey, remember the importance of grit and determination. Embrace failure as a teacher, set audacious goals, and pursue them with unwavering resolve. In doing so, you unlock your full potential and chart a course toward a future defined by success, resilience, and the unyielding pursuit of your passions.

Chapter Nine

Celebrating Success with a Chuckle

Celebrating success is a crucial practice in the journey of personal development. In a world that often encourages you to continually reach for higher goals, it's easy to lose sight of your accomplishments and how far you've come. This chapter emphasizes the importance of taking the time to acknowledge and celebrate both small and significant achievements along the way.

Why Celebrate Success?

Building Achievement on Success: Celebrating success serves as a foundation for future accomplishments. When individuals achieve something, whether it's a promotion, a completed project, or a personal goal, it inspires them to aim even higher. Each success becomes a stepping-stone to the next goal. People are motivated by having a tangible achievement to strive toward, and celebrating these achievements instills confidence and self-belief. Recognizing success reinforces the idea that they can succeed again and sets a positive cycle of personal growth in motion.

Reflecting on Progress: Personal development often encourages you to focus on continuous improvement and setting new goals. While this mindset is valuable, it can also lead to a perpetual sense of striving and dissatisfaction. It's important to occasionally look back and acknowledge how far you've come. Reflecting on your progress can remind you that the journey itself is meaningful, not just the destination. By celebrating milestones, you gain a sense of perspective and resilience that helps you navigate setbacks and challenges.

Mental Health and Resilience: Recognizing and celebrating milestones is not only about acknowledging achievements—it's also about nurturing your mental health and resilience. When you encounter setbacks or face difficulties, knowing that you've overcome obstacles in the past can boost your confidence and motivation. It provides evidence that setbacks are temporary and that you have the strength to overcome them. Celebrating success reinforces a positive mindset and equips you to deal with life's ups and downs more effectively.

Celebrating success is a practice that should be embraced on the personal development journey. It builds a foundation for future achievements, fosters self-confidence, and reminds you of the importance of the journey itself. By acknowledging and celebrating your milestones, you not only boost your mental resilience but also gain a deeper appreciation for your own growth and progress. Success is not just about the destination—it's about recognizing and celebrating the journey along the way.

Physiological Benefits of Celebrating Success

Celebrating success isn't just a mental and emotional boost—it also has physiological advantages. When you acknowledge and feel successful, your body undergo chemical changes that have positive effects on your overall well-being. This natural response can be a powerful motivator and an essential aspect of self-motivation.

Release of Endorphins: Celebrating success triggers the release of endorphins in your brain. Endorphins are neurotransmitters known as "feel-good" chemicals. They interact with receptors in your brain to reduce your perception of pain and trigger positive feelings. The rush of endorphins during moments of celebration makes you feel elated and reinforces your sense of accomplishment.

Reinforcing Success: The experience of feeling successful and the subsequent release of endorphins create a feedback loop. When you celebrate your achievements, it strengthens the neural pathways associated with success and positive emotions. As a result, you become more inclined to pursue success again in the future. This intrinsic motivation drives you to repeat the behaviors and actions that lead to success.

Intrinsic Motivation: Celebrating success, when done effectively, serves as an intrinsic motivator. Intrinsic motivation is the internal drive that compels you to engage in an activity for the sheer joy and satisfaction it brings rather than for external rewards or recognition. When you celebrate your achievements in a meaningful and personally fulfilling way, it reinforces your intrinsic motivation to continue striving for success.

Setting Goals and Defining Success

The concept of success varies from person to person, shaped by individual goals, values, and life circumstances. Defining success is a personal endeavor that aligns with your unique vision for your life. Whether your goals are formally structured or more fluid, having a sense of direction is essential for personal growth and achievement.

Personal Vision: Success begins with a personal vision for where you want to be in life. This vision serves as a guiding light, illuminating your aspirations, desires, and the life you wish to create for yourself. It's a deeply individual perspective that reflects your values, passions, and long-term objectives.

Evolving Goals: Your goals and what you consider success can evolve over time. Life is dynamic, and your priorities may shift as you progress through different stages of life. What you define as success in your early career may differ from what you aspire to achieve in your personal life or later years. Embracing the fluidity of goals allows you to adapt and grow in response to changing circumstances.

Goal Setting: Goals provide the structure and direction needed to turn your vision of success into actionable steps. Whether you set specific, measurable, achievable, relevant, and time-bound (SMART) goals or prefer a more flexible approach, having goals gives you clarity and purpose. They serve as milestones on your journey toward your personal definition of success.

Celebrating success not only has psychological benefits but also triggers physiological changes in your body. It reinforces your motivation, making you more likely to pursue success in the future. Defining success is a deeply personal process that aligns with your vision and goals, which may evolve over time. Setting goals provides a roadmap for achieving your aspirations and realizing your unique version of success at different stages of life.

Celebrating vs. Rewarding

Celebrating your success and rewarding yourself may seem similar, but they serve different purposes and tap into distinct forms of motivation. Understanding the nuances of these approaches enables you to harness the power of both in your personal development journey.

Rewarding Yourself: The Endpoint Achievement

Rewarding yourself signifies reaching the culmination of a process, indicating that you have successfully met your goal and are deserving of a prize or recognition. It emphasizes the final outcome, marking the completion of a task or accomplishment. Rewards can take various forms, such as gifts, trophies, ribbons, or monetary incentives.

- **Extrinsic Motivation:** Rewards are often associated with extrinsic motivation, where the driving force behind completing a task is the anticipation of an external reward. People motivated extrinsically are focused on the tangible benefits or recognition they will receive at the end of their efforts. The process itself may become secondary to the ultimate prize.

- **Potential Drawback:** Overreliance on extrinsic motivation and rewards can pose challenges. When individuals become accustomed to external incentives, their intrinsic motivation to engage in the task may diminish. Once the external reward is removed, they may struggle to find the same level of energy and enthusiasm for the task.

Celebrating Success: Embracing the Journey

Celebrating success is distinct from rewarding yourself in that it revolves around appreciating the entire process and journey of achievement. It emphasizes the effort, growth, and learning that occur along the way rather than solely focusing on the end result. Celebration infuses positive emotions into the effort invested in reaching a goal.

- **Intrinsic Motivation:** Celebration often aligns with intrinsic motivation, where the motivation to engage in a task arises from within. Intrinsically motivated individuals find joy and fulfillment in the process itself, regardless of external rewards or outcomes. They derive satisfaction from the act of doing and growing.

- **Enhancing Intrinsic Motivation:** Healthy celebration of success can enhance intrinsic motivation. By acknowledging and appreciating the effort and progress made, individuals reinforce the positive emotions associated with their pursuits. This, in turn, fuels their internal motivation to continue engaging in similar tasks or challenges for the sheer pleasure of the journey.

In summary, while celebrating success and rewarding yourself both mark achievements, they cater to different motivational aspects. Rewarding signifies reaching an endpoint and is often tied to extrinsic motivation. In contrast, celebrating emphasizes the journey, nurtures intrinsic motivation, and promotes a deeper appreciation for the process. Balancing both approaches allows you to harness the dual forces of external recognition and internal joy, ultimately enhancing your personal development journey.

Celebrating Success in a Healthy Way

Celebrating your success is a vital part of your personal development journey. It not only acknowledges your achievements but also fuels your motivation to keep moving forward. Here are some simple and healthy ways to celebrate your success:

Journal Your Progress: Take the time to journal your progress, even if you haven't reached your ultimate goal yet. Reflect on how far you've come and the milestones you've achieved along the way. This practice helps you stay positive and maintain the momentum necessary for continued success.

Include Others: Don't forget the people who have supported you on your journey. Celebrate your success by including your supporters in your festivities. Consider organizing a special dinner or gathering to express your gratitude. Be specific about what you value in each person, making them feel genuinely appreciated. Nurturing meaningful relationships with your supporters encourages them to continue helping you in the future.

Take Time for Yourself: Rest and self-care are essential. When you've accomplished something significant, it's an ideal time to take a day off to recharge. Celebrate in ways that nourish your mind, body, and spirit. Choose activities that resonate with your interests and preferences. This could include hosting a dinner party, taking a leisurely walk or jog in the park, watching a beautiful sunrise or sunset, indulging in a massage or spa treatment, having a game night with friends, starting a new journal, embarking on an adventure, or exploring a new hobby. Spending quality time alone allows you to reflect on your achievements and recharge for what lies ahead.

Reflect: Celebrating success goes beyond acknowledging the end result; it involves reflecting on the journey you undertook to reach your goal. Use the following questions to guide your reflection:

- What aspects of this journey did I enjoy the most?
- In what areas did I excel?
- What strengths did I leverage?
- What new skills did I acquire?
- Which accomplishments boosted my confidence?
- How did I overcome obstacles along the way?
- What changes would I consider for the future?

Taking the time to reflect provides valuable insights into your strengths and how to utilize them for future successes. It allows you to process your experience and gain a deeper understanding of yourself.

Celebrating success is not just a momentary indulgence; it's a way to honor your progress, appreciate your supporters, and gain clarity on your journey. So, go ahead and celebrate your achievements in a healthy and meaningful way, knowing that each milestone brings you closer to your goals.

Embrace Self-Care for Your Well-Deserved Break

Achieving your goals is undoubtedly demanding and often requires inner strength. Amid the hustle and bustle of progress, it's easy to overlook the need for self-care. When you reach a milestone or conquer a particularly challenging task, it's essential to pause and indulge in self-care. Whether it's savoring a great cup of coffee, finding a moment of solitude, or engaging in self-reflection, these moments of relaxation are crucial. They serve as a celebration of your success and a means to rejuvenate your spirit for the journey ahead.

Revel in Quality Time with Loved Ones

Family and close relationships often can provide you with your ultimate purpose in life. When you transform your "shoulds" into "musts," you connect your goals to this fundamental purpose. Therefore, when it's time to celebrate your achievements, you naturally turn to your loved ones. Observing the positive impact your success has on your nearest and dearest is profoundly inspiring. It fuels your determination to persist and achieve even more, knowing that your accomplishments bring joy to those you cherish.

Express Your Gratitude

No one attains success entirely on their own; mentors and supporters play pivotal roles. Celebrate your success by showing appreciation to those who have aided your journey. Consider a delightful dinner outing or heartfelt tokens of gratitude. Express your heartfelt sentiments and let them know how much their support means to you. In the grand tapestry of life, giving back and sharing your accomplishments with others, even as you celebrate your own, is a profound aspect of living fully.

Get Creative and Move Your Body

Celebration can take the form of victory dances. These expressive movements can boost confidence and energize you in unique ways. The next time you reach a goal, crank up your favorite song and dance with abandon. Strike a powerful pose, practice yoga, or simply take a leisurely walk outdoors. These physical expressions of joy serve a dual purpose: they allow you to celebrate success and elevate your mood, infusing you with renewed vigor.

Cultivate Gratitude and Set New Intentions

Practicing gratitude is an ongoing journey, and it's particularly impactful after significant achievements. Take a deep, purposeful breath to savor the feelings of relief, happiness, or excitement that your success brings. Simultaneously, set your intentions for what comes next. This powerful combination allows you to celebrate your achievements while channeling your energy toward fresh goals on the horizon.

Embrace Spontaneity

While goal-oriented planning is essential, a touch of spontaneity can invigorate your life. Celebrate your success by stepping out of your comfort zone and embracing spontaneity. Share the moment with someone you care about, and let go of rigid plans. Allow the day to unfold naturally, exploring uncharted experiences that bring excitement and variety to your journey.

Use Success as Fuel for Future Goals

Success isn't just a destination; it's also the fuel that propels you forward. Regardless of the scale of your accomplishments, always take the time to celebrate them. Track your progress diligently, acknowledging how far you've come, even if your ultimate goal remains ahead. Celebrating your achievements keeps your spirits high and serves as the driving force for continued success on your path.

Enjoy the Journey

Having a vision for the future is not only great but also crucial. It serves as your guiding star, helping you navigate life's journey and make significant decisions. However, there's a fine line between aspiring for the future and becoming so consumed by it that you forget to savor the present.

Sometimes, in your relentless pursuit of your goals, you lose touch with the simple joys of life. The journey becomes a daunting ordeal, and you begin to believe that your happiness is contingent on distant life circumstances. While you should always pursue your ambitions, dreams, and aspirations, it's essential to remember that once a day is over, you can't retrieve that time.

As you fast forward five or ten years down the road, ensure you can look back with joy at the wonderful memories you've created along the way. Maya Angelou's beautiful words reminds us, "Life is not measured by the number of breaths you take but by the moments that take your breath away."

It's equally vital for your happiness and success to strike a balance between living for today and planning for tomorrow. So, slow down and immerse yourself in the beauty that surrounds you right now. Here are a few tips to help you relish the journey, especially if you're feeling disheartened and struggling with patience.

You Have Permission to Have Fun

Life can become overwhelmingly busy. Your days are filled with obligations and responsibilities, leaving you feeling like you're in a race against the clock. It's challenging to find time for yourself, let alone allocate this precious time for "irresponsible" fun. However, that might be precisely what you need.

Ask yourself, "What do I want to do today? What would genuinely increase my happiness?" Then, grant yourself permission to indulge in something you truly enjoy. As actor and director Michael Landon Jr. wisely advises, "Do it! I say. Whatever you want to do, do it now! There are only so many tomorrows."

Focus on Progress and Celebrate Small Victories

While you may not have reached your ultimate destination in life, it's likely that you've made significant progress compared to where you were a few years ago. Achieving the desired results and personal growth that supports these outcomes is an ongoing process, possibly a lifelong journey.

Take a moment to acknowledge how far you've come in life and credit yourself for your efforts along the way. It's effortless to fixate on the work still ahead of you and overlook the progress you've achieved. Celebrate the small wins and successes that adorn your life today. Give yourself the recognition you deserve as you continue to work toward changing the world. It's no small feat, and your journey is worth cherishing every step of the way.

Embracing Challenges, Risks, and Mistakes: Finding Joy in the Journey

In the course of any journey, challenges and obstacles are bound to arise. Unfortunately, many individuals view these hurdles not as natural occurrences but as reasons to throw in the towel.

However, if you truly want to savor the journey, it's essential to shift your perspective. Learn to relish challenges and embrace risks with an open heart. Step into the unknown with curiosity and intrigue, recognizing that mistakes are not roadblocks but stepping-stones, offering valuable lessons along the way.

The wise words of Louisa May Alcott remind us, "I am not afraid of storms for I am learning how to sail my ship." The author of *Little Women* believed that challenges are the storms that test your mettle, and by navigating them, you become a better captain of your own destiny.

Slow and Steady Wins the Race

In your quest for personal growth and life improvement, the notion of slowing down may appear counterintuitive. Why not charge forward, achieving your goals as swiftly as possible? The allure of rapid progress is undeniable, but it can often lead to burnout and frustration.

Sometimes, the most profound clarity and the richest experiences are found in the moments when you slow down. The relentless pursuit of achieving more and doing it faster can rob you of the joy of the journey. It's in these frenzied states that you may overlook the simple pleasures and profound lessons that each step along the way can offer.

Instead, consider taking a breather, focusing on the next best step, and immersing yourself fully in the present moment. Embrace the journey, relish every step, and find delight in the process of learning and growth. Stay curious about what today has to offer, and you'll discover that the journey itself becomes a source of immense satisfaction and fulfillment.

The Journey Teaches You to Be Adaptable

When embarking on the path toward a Big Goal, it's essential to acknowledge that the journey will rarely be a linear one. Along the way, there will be bumps and obstacles that may seem like roadblocks, but in reality, they are your most valuable teachers. These challenges impart crucial life skills—flexibility and adaptability.

For those who seek a smooth and obstacle-free life journey, it's entirely possible to craft such an existence. However, it's important to understand that these bumps and obstacles serve a profound purpose: they instruct you in the art of flexibility and adaptability.

Consider this: During her high school years, Stacy set her sights on the ambitious goal of obtaining a college degree. Unfortunately, the United States is known for its expensive higher education system, and her family's financial situation can't support her studying at an American college. Rather than letting this financial hurdle thwart her dreams, Stacy chooses to pivot. She applies to and is accepted by a university in Canada, where the cost of education is substantially lower. This decision not only enables her to acquire an excellent education but also enriches her life with diverse experiences.

In pursuit of my goal, Stacy had to demonstrate flexibility. She refused to surrender her dream, even when faced with financial constraints, and instead adapted by seeking an alternative path to my desired destination. Stacy embraced the opportunity to study in another country, far from home, and gained valuable life experiences in the process.

The valuable lessons in flexibility and adaptability that she learned during that journey will continue to serve her throughout her life. Whenever she sets her sights on a Big Goal, she is prepared to make the necessary adjustments and embrace any twists and turns that come her way.

Conclusion

In conclusion, it's important to remember that while achieving the destination is undoubtedly significant, the journey itself holds immeasurable value. Growth, learning, and fulfillment flourish along the path toward a Big Goal. Thus, it's crucial to find joy in the journey and recognize that every step taken is a lesson learned and a skill honed.

When you reach your goals, celebrate them. Enjoy every step, and acknowledge every milestone. This sometimes means taking a break and consciously stepping away for a moment. Burning yourself out by pushing yourself past your limits isn't going to get you to your destination any quicker. Instead, you're going to grow distant from your objective, hating the tasks at hand and digging yourself into a pit of frustration. A pit that can take a while to get out of.

So, take your time and move at your own pace. Dance when you want to dance and laugh when you want to laugh. Set yourself up for success by setting manageable objectives. If the project starts going in a new direction, go with it. Be adaptable and allow the path to move as it needs to. Remember, you have permission to have fun.

As you embark on your journey toward your goals and aspirations, celebrate the process. Embrace each challenge as an opportunity to cultivate flexibility and adaptability—skills that will not only aid you in achieving your current goal but will also empower you to conquer countless others in the future.

Chapter Ten

Take Risks and Make Sh** Happen

Dear reader, it's time to talk about something that can make the difference between a life lived in monotony and a life bursting with adventure, growth, and unforgettable moments: taking risks.

The Comfort Zone: A Safe Haven or a Trap?

You can often find comfort in your routine, your familiar surroundings, and the predictability of your daily life. The comfort zone, as it's aptly named, is a cozy place where everything feels safe and known. But here's the catch: too much comfort can lead to stagnation.

Think about it. When was the last time you experienced that electrifying rush of adrenaline, the butterflies in your stomach, and the thrill of stepping into the unknown? Those are the moments when life truly comes alive.

Risk-Taking: The Fuel for Progress

Taking risks isn't just a daredevil's game; it's the driving force behind progress and innovation. It's the spark that ignites creativity, resilience, and the thirst for new horizons. But more than that, it's the magic ingredient that turns dreams into reality.

Risk-Taking: A Path to Growth

Every risk you take, no matter the outcome, is a valuable lesson. Whether you soar to success or stumble into failure, you're learning, adapting, and growing. Those who dare to take risks are the ones who evolve, not just in their careers but in their personal lives as well.

Imagine the first time you tried to ride a bicycle. You wobbled, you fell, but you got up and tried again. Eventually, you mastered it, and that feeling of accomplishment was worth every scraped knee. Life's risks are no different. Embrace them, learn from them, and watch yourself soar.

Turning Dreams into Reality

Remember those big dreams you tucked away, thinking they were too grand, too audacious to pursue? Well, it's time to dust them off. Taking risks is the bridge between dreaming and doing. It's the audacity to say, "I'm going for it."

Whether you dream of starting a business, traveling the world, or making a difference in your community, taking calculated risks is the key to turning those dreams into tangible, awe-inspiring realities. Don't let the fear of the unknown hold you back; let it propel you forward.

Do Not Live a Life Full of Regrets!

When you look back on your life, will you regret the risks you took or the opportunities you missed? Regret is a heavy burden, one that stems from letting fear dictate your choices. But here's the secret: you have the power to regret-proof your life.

Imagine the stories you'll tell, the adventures you'll recount, and the moments that will make you smile as you look back. Those stories are waiting for you on the other side of risk-taking. Seize them with both hands and cherish them as the tapestry of your extraordinary life.

The Art of Taking Calculated Risks

Now, taking risks doesn't mean throwing caution to the wind. It's about making informed, calculated decisions. Here are a few tips to help you navigate the world of risk-taking:

Define Your Goals: Clearly understand what you want to achieve. Clarity will guide your decisions.

Assess the Risk: Evaluate the potential outcomes, both positive and negative. What's the worst that can happen? Can you handle it?

Plan Strategically: Develop a well-thought-out plan to mitigate potential pitfalls and maximize your chances of success.

Seek Knowledge: Equip yourself with knowledge and skills relevant to your endeavor. The more you know, the better your decisions.

Embrace Failure: Understand that setbacks are part of the journey. Failure is not the end; it's a stepping-stone to success.

Your Call to Action

As you read these words, envision your life a year from now, five years from now, or even a decade from now. Do you see a life colored by remarkable experiences, bold choices, and breathtaking achievements?

The power to make that vision a reality lies within you. It starts with a single step—a risk taken, a dream pursued, a leap of faith. Don't let the fear of the unknown hold you back. Instead, let it be the fuel that propels you forward into the adventure of a lifetime.

Challenge yourself. Embrace the unknown, take calculated risks, and make sh** happen. Your extraordinary journey awaits, and it begins with that daring step into the realm of possibilities.

As you close this book, remember this: life is too short to play it safe. Take risks, seize opportunities, and create the life you've always dreamed of. Your destiny is calling. Answer it with courage, enthusiasm, and the unwavering belief that your dreams are worth fighting for.

The Unfinished Story

You've come this far, and I applaud you for it. You haven't simply purchased this book and left it to collect dust on your nightstand. No, you've delved into its chapters, absorbed its wisdom, and explored its lessons. And for that, I want to extend my deepest gratitude.

But here's the thing: our journey together isn't complete just yet. You see, knowledge is a powerful tool, but it remains dormant until we breathe life into it through action. It's like having a treasure map but never embarking on the adventure to find the hidden riches.

Lessons to Live By

Throughout this book, you've encountered a wealth of insights, strategies, and stories meant to inspire, motivate, and empower you. These pages are filled with lessons that can transform your life, both personally and professionally. But these lessons are not mere words on paper; they are invitations to take action.

Think of this book as a toolbox. You've unlocked it, and now it's time to pick up the tools and put them to work. Let the lessons you've learned become the foundation upon which you build a brighter, more fulfilling future.

The Ripple Effect

One of the most beautiful aspects of personal growth and self-improvement is its ripple effect. When you apply the lessons from this book to your life, you not only enhance your own journey but also inspire those around you. Your actions become a testament to the power of transformation.

Imagine the impact you can have on your friends, family, colleagues, and even strangers as they witness your growth and success. Your journey can ignite a spark in others, encouraging them to embark on their paths of self-discovery and achievement.

Your Commitment to Excellence

You've shown a commitment to excellence by reading this book and seeking knowledge that can enrich your life. Now, it's time to take that commitment to the next level by applying what you've learned. It's time to turn knowledge into wisdom and wisdom into action.

As you move forward, remember that progress is a journey, not a destination. Be patient with yourself, embrace the setbacks as learning opportunities, and celebrate every small victory along the way. Your journey is unique, and every step you take is a testament to your determination and resilience.

The Journey Continues

As we reach the end of this chapter, I want to leave you with a simple yet profound message: the journey continues. Your life story is an ongoing narrative filled with twists, turns, challenges, and triumphs. This book is just one chapter in that story, and I'm excited to see how the rest unfolds.

Thank you for being a part of this journey. Thank you for investing in your personal growth. Thank you for believing in the power of transformation. And thank you for not just reading this book but for embracing its lessons and using them to create a life filled with purpose, fulfillment, and joy.

With heartfelt gratitude,

Deborah LeBlanc

Don't allow your dreams to stay dreams. It's time to boost your brainpower...

Dr. Deborah LeBlanc's *Make Sh** Happen* is a call to action for dreamers stuck in neutral. Consider this book the first stepping stone on your pathway toward true accomplishment.

Inside, you'll discover a treasure trove of wisdom, from myth-busting science to productivity hacks that make progress feel like playtime. You'll map your trajectory by way of insightful exercises, then watch your efficiency soar—at last. With witty warmth and cold hard facts, this little book will make a big difference, facilitating a mindset shift that's guaranteed to take you off the sofa and test your limits.

The outcome? A life you've only imagined—a life you've never dared to claim. It's time to cut through the nasty habits, endless excuses, and sloppy plans. It's time to work smart instead of hard. It's time to make sh** happen!

About the Author

Deborah LeBlanc is a Certified Clinical Hypnotherapist with certifications in ten other healing modalities that span over seventy presenting issues. Her expertise in relationship building has afforded her the opportunity to travel throughout the country as a keynote speaker and workshop facilitator.

www.ingramcontent.com/pod-product-compliance
Lightning Source LLC
Chambersburg PA
CBHW070109080526
44586CB00013B/1236